USING HOME LANGUAGE

AS A RESOURCE IN THE CLASSROOM

A GUIDE FOR TEACHERS OF ENGLISH LEARNERS

KATE PATERSON

www.tesol.org/bookstore

TESOL International Association
1925 Ballenger Avenue
Alexandria, VA 22314 USA
www.tesol.org

Group Director, Content and Learning: Myrna Jacobs
Copy Editor: Tomiko Breland, Allison Rainville
Production Editor: Tomiko Breland
Manuscript Reviewers: Robyn Brinks Lockwood, Gilda Martinez-Alba
Cover Design: Citrine Sky Design
Design and Layout: Capitol Communications, LLC

Recommended citation:

Paterson, K. (2021). *Using home language as a resource in the classroom: A guide for teachers
of English learners*. TESOL International Association.

ISBN 978-1-945351-96-9
ISBN (ebook) 978-1-945351-97-6
Library of Congress Control Number 2021936798

CONTENTS

Chapter 4
Moving Toward a More Equitable Future 75

References and Further Reading 85

Indexes, Appendixes, and Resources 95

INTRODUCTION

"Language is inextricably linked to students' identities, experiences and, most importantly, opportunities to learn."

Jacqueline D'warte (2014, p. 22)

An educator's role is multifaceted; we are resources, collaborators, role models, leaders, and lifelong learners. We play an impactful role in the relationship students develop with school. What we do in the classroom profoundly influences students' attitudes toward learning, how they see themselves as learners, and how much of themselves they choose to invest in school.

As professionals, we continually reflect on our practice and ask critical questions. Am I serving my students well? Do they feel included, valued, and capable? How can I expand my knowledge and deepen my understanding to ensure I am providing optimal learning conditions for everyone? This guidebook was written to facilitate and extend this meaningful dialogue. Its central purpose is to address one of the most pressing questions teachers are asking themselves today: What can I do right now, in my own classroom, to support students of varied cultures and languages in thriving and achieving, both academically and personally? In an era of unprecedented cultural and linguistic diversity, formulating innovative answers to this question is imperative.

There are currently more than seven million English learners (ELs) in schools in the United States and Canada today—a number that continues to rise (National Center for Education Statistics, 2020; Statistics Canada, 2020). The goal of *Using Home Language as a Resource in the Classroom* is to assist educators in supporting this growing, yet underserved, student demographic by drawing on their rich and complex linguistic repertoires as valuable resources for learning. Generally absent from professional discourse, the vital role for home language (L1) in supporting additional language (L2) and content learning at school has been documented by a large and comprehensive body of research. The monolingual (English-only) instructional principles that currently dominate English as a second language (ESL) and mainstream K–12 classroom teaching are inconsistent with current understandings about the ways in which we learn. This book addresses this troubling research-to-practice gap by making connections between what we *know* (empirical evidence that establishes L1 as being essential to students' success) and what we *do* (teaching that predominantly excludes students' L1) every day in the classroom, linking the most up-to-date knowledge about language learning and bilingualism with actual instructional practice. This guide outlines what teachers need to know to orchestrate evidence-based instruction for ELs and bilingual students and offers guidance—teaching strategies, in-class activities, and lesson ideas—on how to make those understandings actionable in the classroom.

Who Is This Guide For?

The primary audience for this guide is current and future teachers of ELs across various educational and geographical settings. This includes preservice, novice, and experienced teachers; those providing direct English language instruction (e.g., ESL teachers), those in bilingual programs (transitional as well as dual-language education); and generalist or subject-area grade-level teachers in mainstream K–12 schools—the majority of whom count ELs among their student ranks. Though many of the teaching resources in this book have been aligned with K–12 Common Core State Standards in the United States, the teaching strategies, lesson ideas, classroom activities, and online resources (throughout and in Appendix A) found within these pages can be readily adapted to other educational contexts, including adult, postsecondary, foreign language, and immersion programs. In addition to being applicable across varied classroom contexts, the inclusion of L1 in teaching and learning is relevant in increasingly diverse and multilingual classrooms across the globe.

Whether you are an ESL instructor, a high school science teacher, a college professor, or a provider of literacy support in elementary school, your instructional decisions impact how successfully the ELs in your classroom develop English language and literacy skills and meet content standards. This guide encourages you not to approach this work as a challenge but as an opportunity. It advocates for adopting a language-as-resource rather than a language-as-problem mindset. It challenges you to critically reflect on how you think about and act on ELs' language practices both inside and outside of the classroom.

Though the principal audience for this book is educators, there is much within these covers for policymakers, administrators, teacher educators, curriculum designers, and materials developers to consider when making decisions around what matters in promoting academic success among learners of English at school. If administrators incorporate accountability for ELs more broadly throughout the school district, for example, and make it clear that everyone is responsible for the success of ELs—not exclusively EL teachers and EL department staff—it spurs collaboration and aligns various stakeholders in common purpose. If principals are sufficiently knowledgeable on effective instruction for ELs, they can make more informed policy decisions around which language support program(s) they will implement in their school. If school leaders provide all teaching staff, not just EL support personnel, with professional development on effective instruction of ELs, the result will be greater access to general education curriculum and resources for these students. If curriculum designers and materials developers understand the value of students' L1 in enhancing classroom learning for all students, we will begin to see changes in classroom resources that promote inclusion and more efficient learning—materials that support the development of both L1 and English for ELs and promote metalinguistic awareness and intercultural competence for everyone.

Why Is This Guide Needed?

In English-medium K–12 schools, more teachers than ever before are providing direct instruction to ELs. The majority of ELs are placed in mainstream classrooms for at least part of their school day and are expected to learn the same academic content as their native-English-speaking peers. The success of these students is a shared responsibility; it is not solely the job of ESL or bilingual teachers to promote language and literacy development at school. However, broad support for ELs in K–12 schools is impeded by the fact that many teachers, as well as administrators (e.g., principals, vice principals) and support personnel (e.g., guidance counselors, literacy specialists, special education aides), have not had training or professional development focused on appropriate instruction for a linguistically diverse student body. Generally speaking, there is no significant expectation or requirement for educators or school leaders to be familiar with the knowledge base pertaining to effective instruction for ELs. Many teachers report low self-efficacy and a lack of preparedness to teach these students effectively (Durgunoglu & Hughes, 2010; Moore, 2014). This is problematic in light of continually increasing numbers of ELs in classrooms across the United States and their consistently poor academic outcomes in comparison to non-ELs. As Sanchez (2017) summarizes:

> Many ELLs [English language learners] remain stuck in academically segregated programs where they fall behind in basic subjects. Only 63 percent of ELLs graduate from high school, compared with the overall national rate of 82 percent. In New York State, for example, the overall high school graduation rate is about 78 percent. But for ELLs, it's 37 percent, according to the National Center for Education Statistics. Of those who do graduate, only 1.4 percent take college entrance exams. (p. 8)

Research findings across numerous school districts show that ELs both at the elementary level in ESL pullout programs and at the secondary level who are taking ESL as a subject frequently fail to catch up to their same-age peers. The sizable achievement gap between ELs and non-ELs shows no signs of narrowing (Murphy, 2014; U.S. Department of Education, 2018).

The status quo is not working. Schools are in dire need of instructional practices that promote greater inclusion and educational equity for these students. It is important to note, however, that although this book focuses on teachers and their unique opportunity to make a positive difference in the schooling experiences of ELs, they cannot go it alone. Enduring change will need to involve multiple levels of the educational system as well as organizations in the public and private sector.

Outside of the mainstream K–12 context (e.g., in ESL classrooms where the instructors have been specially trained to deliver English language instruction), English-only policies remain the norm. Traditionally, teaching English to speakers of other languages training programs make little to no mention of students' L1, other than to advise minimizing its use. The ideal classroom is portrayed "as having as little of students' L1 as possible, essentially by omitting reference to it" (Cook, 2001, p. 404). Permitting ELs to explicitly draw on their L1 to support their English language learning is generally the exception and not the rule in ESL learning environments, despite comprehensive empirical evidence that demonstrates the benefits of L1 inclusion, including (but not limited to) improved academic outcomes. If we problematize some of the core assumptions that underlie monolingual language teaching, we can begin to move toward normalizing more flexible language pedagogies that value students' prior knowledge, including their L1, and build upon it to support classroom learning. Moreover, we can start to shift our focus away from trying to create individuals who as closely as possible resemble monolingual native English speakers and instead strive to produce multicompetent bilinguals. For many of us, this may involve changing both the way we teach and the standards we use to evaluate success.

How to Make the Most of This Guide

To make the guide as useful and accessible as possible, the following three types of information have been singled out for easy access. Look for these graphic features:

 PRACTICE: Practical strategies, lessons, in-class activities, and culminating projects that use students' L1 to enrich learning.

 REFLECT: Guiding questions meant to challenge you to think more deeply about what you do in the classroom and why you do it. These questions can be answered independently or be used as talking points in a professional development or teacher education session.

 INSIGHT: Key insights from teachers, students, and scholars. These quotes and bits of wisdom are meant to inspire and deepen understanding on important aspects of this issue.

> Online resources can be found on the companion site for this book, www.tesol.org/homelanguage.

Chapter Overview

This guide is organized in four chapters:

Chapter 1: Evidence-Based Teaching and Social Justice: Why Home Language Is Essential to Student Success compares four common assumptions underlying English-only classroom policy with what the best evidence tells us about the role of L1 in instruction. Examining one's own assumptions and beliefs about teaching and students, individually and collectively, is a crucial part of a teacher's reflection on practice; this is just as true for experienced teachers as it is for new or prospective teachers.

Chapter 1 discusses how to create more equitable educational opportunities for ELs by delivering asset-based instruction and disrupting uneven power relations in the classroom and broader society. When we have critical conversations about how what is valued at school is not the best or only way of knowing and being and extend the curriculum to reflect all students' lives and experiences, we come closer to enacting socially just pedagogy.

Chapter 2: Out of Minds and Into Classroom Spaces: When, How, and How Much Home Language to Incorporate Into Instruction discusses how to bring L1 out of the minds of students and into classroom learning. By acknowledging the cross-lingual connections students are already making in their minds, we can partner with them in applying these strategies more efficiently, in ways that align with academic objectives. This chapter addresses the practical issues of when, how, and how much L1 to integrate into day-to-day instruction and describes ways we can engage with students' digital realities to support language development.

Chapter 3: Home Language and TESOL's *The 6 Principles for Exemplary Teaching of English Learners*® considers the role of L1 in the context of TESOL's 6 Principles. TESOL International Association—a global leader in English language teaching—defines a set of six core tenets and related practices that promote optimal instruction in any classroom that has students who are learning English as a new language: (1) know your learners, (2) create conditions for language learning, (3) design high-quality lessons for language development, (4) adapt lesson delivery as needed, (5) monitor and assess student progress, and (6) engage and collaborate within a community of practice. This chapter describes how L1 can play a pivotal role in helping teachers to implement The 6 Principles in practice.

Chapter 4: Moving Toward a More Equitable Future explains the monolingual native speaker bias and its role in how we view ELs and perceive their success in using language. The chapter explores why and how to integrate positive L2 user role models and examples of L2 user speech into instruction. Teachers of any subject, whether monolingual or polyglot, can embrace a plurilingual orientation that respects and valorizes language practices that lie outside of what is expected at school. Plurilingualism refers to an individual's interconnected knowledge of more than one language and includes "unbalanced" proficiencies or partial skills. A plurilingual orientation in the classroom views all languages and their cultural dimensions as resources for learning; it is a way of thinking and acting that moves us toward a more just educational future.

A Note on Terms

The terminology in the field of English language teaching varies widely and has been hotly debated in the academic literature. The terms we use matter; language is intimately connected with thought and thought with action. It is important to be transparent about the choices we make. With this in mind, the key terms used in this guide are explicated as follows:

Mother tongue or *native/first/home language* have all been used to refer to the language a person is most comfortable using (often the language learned in childhood and spoken at home). Practically speaking, these terms can fail to reflect the complex linguistic backgrounds of many of our students. The language a person learned first may not be the same language they are most comfortable with now, or they may have multiple languages that they identify as being their L1. Moreover, a person's most fluent language may not be the one with which they associate their ethnolinguistic identity (Laakso & Sarhimaa, 2016). Terms like *first* and *second language* are also problematic because they imply that languages are sequentially acquired and operate autonomously inside a bilingual's mind. Extensive evidence shows that this is not, in fact, the case (Grosjean, 1989; Cummins, 2007a; García, Lin et al., 2017).

Much of the language we use around ELs is deficit based. Policy and curriculum documents often refer to the "challenges" these students present in the classroom. The term *English learner* itself, as well as other commonly used terms, like *limited English proficient*, define students by what they are perceived to be lacking—namely, adequate English proficiency. These labels have been widely criticized for devaluing the linguistic and cultural knowledge that students bring into the classroom. Educational researchers, teachers, and students alike have proposed alternatives, for example, "multilingual students" as petitioned by students at Seven Hills Charter School (2015) or "emergent bilinguals" as used by García (2009), that highlight the linguistic accomplishments of students rather than their presumed limitations.

The terms *home language* (L1), *additional language* (L2), *English as a second language* (ESL), and *English learner* (EL) are used throughout this guidebook because they are the ones most frequently used in official policy and curriculum documents as well as among educators. The target audience here is teachers. For the sake of clarity and to make content as accessible as possible, I chose recognizable terms, with the important caveat that these labels have potentially harmful connotations. It is a central tenet of this guide that ELs come to class already in possession of valuable resources for learning. The practical applications in this guide are seated in an evidence-based understanding of languages as interconnected parts of a unified whole inside a bilingual's mind. I hope that in the future, terms that better reflect these realities will be standard—codified in official education documents and routinely used in professional discourse.

Additionally, though I use the term *EL* throughout, the content and practice suggestions included in this book are relevant not just to students identified as ELs but also to those who have transitioned out of language support programs and bilingual students who grew up speaking both English and language(s) other than English at home.

Moving Forward

The English language can act as a significant barrier for ELs in being able to demonstrate what they can do and the unique ways they can do it. Teachers can struggle to make content comprehensible and provide pathways for ELs to participate fully, exercise creativity, and engage in cognitively challenging work. L1 can be used as a resource in any subject at any time when English is a barrier to accessing meaning and its construction. If a student's English proficiency is insufficient for carrying out a classroom task, their L1 can make it possible for them to understand the instructions, grapple with the texts being used, and participate in the activity in order to develop knowledge and experience without waiting. Permitting a student to learn by achieving the objectives of the task regardless of their level in the language of instruction means that as they meet the challenges of learning a new language, they do not fall progressively further behind in the curriculum.

You do not need to be bilingual to implement bilingual teaching strategies and orchestrate culturally sustaining pedagogy. This book provides guidance on how to utilize students' L1s in service of learning regardless of your own language background.

As teachers, we influence whether ELs feel pride in their emerging bilingualism or shame and embarrassment in perceived deficits in English proficiency. How *we* view and respond to their L1 and all of the knowledge and experience encoded within influences how *they* view their value and potential at school. We are a consequential part of whether ELs develop the bilingual and biliteracy skills and identities that they so critically need to succeed. Having an openly multilingual classroom means that rather than oversimplifying and watering down our instruction, we can teach cognitively challenging content because we have permitted all students access to all of their resources for learning. We can maintain high expectations for everyone in our classroom, including our multicompetent ELs.

CHAPTER 1

EVIDENCE-BASED TEACHING AND SOCIAL JUSTICE: WHY HOME LANGUAGE IS ESSENTIAL TO STUDENT SUCCESS

Any teacher that is using English as the medium of instruction and teaching to a linguistically diverse student group makes consequential decisions about how to convey information and assess learning in the course of each school day. Language is the instrument we use to explain, communicate task and learning objectives, evaluate progress, and provide feedback in the classroom. We require students to read and comprehend academic texts in various subject areas, produce written assignments, and interact with peers and teachers—all through the language of instruction. To succeed in English-medium schools, students must be able to access the curriculum and demonstrate learning through English. So, although it is true for all students that language cannot be separated from what is learned and taught in school, this fact carries special weight for English learners (ELs). Because they are learning English and simultaneously learning the content of the curriculum through English, the process of language learning is intertwined in complex ways with all of their school learning.

This chapter provides a foundational knowledge base for understanding why home language (L1) is essential to ELs' success at school. I begin by describing four interrelated assumptions that underlie English-only instruction and comparing them with related research-based evidence. Breaking down misconceptions about language teaching is crucial if we are to orchestrate instruction that enables equitable access to education for linguistically diverse students. Next, L1 is discussed in terms of the opportunities it generates to counter deficit narratives, affirm student identities, and push back against broader educational and societal inequities. This knowledge and its related instructional implications are inextricably linked to social justice. Finally, though it is critical that our teaching practices are evidence based and informed by a desire to effect positive change, it is equally important that we have the tools to make our knowledge and intentions actionable in the classroom. Practice ideas with lessons and activities related to discussion points are included throughout the chapter.

Do you think it is important for ELs to maintain and develop their L1 as they learn English? If so, why? If not, why not? Return to this question when you have finished reading this guidebook. Notice and reflect on any changes to your original position.

Language Learning: Assumptions vs. Evidence

Consider which, if any, of the following beliefs you hold to be true. Do you have ambivalent feelings about any? An inherent part of being an effective teacher is reflecting on practice; this includes critically examining the assumptions, judgements, and expectations we bring with us into the classroom.

Assumption #1

Learning two or more languages will negatively affect a child's development in both languages.

Evidence: The English-only or English-as-soon-as-possible orientation of most schools partly derives from the fact that many parents and educators regard English as the language of success, in both school and life, and assume that actively developing language and literacy skills in a child's L1 will come at the expense of English language and literacy skills. However, there is no evidence to support this. What the research does show is that students who have their L1 acknowledged and built upon in school are likely to outperform their same-age peers in English-only environments and experience greater academic achievement (August & Shanahan, 2006). This is because the academic language and literacy skills that students develop in their L1 readily transfer to English (Cummins, 2005). If students are already literate in a language other than English, many of the skills they developed to help them learn to read and write in that language will help them as they learn to read and write in English (e.g., sound-symbol correspondence, figuring out meaning from context).

Teaching students to read in their L1 improves their reading abilities in English (Bourgoin, 2014; Cummins, 1991b; Sparks et al., 2012). This is evident in long-term studies by Thomas and Collier (2002, 2004) where ELs in bilingual programs outperformed their counterparts in monolingual English programs after between 4 to 7 years of dual-language instruction. ELs in English-only programs, on the other hand, rarely achieved grade-level expectations when compared to their native-English-speaking classmates. By Grade 5, the ELs in mainstream English-only programs exhibited significant reading and math deficits compared to ELs that received language support that included use of their L1.

The benefits of L1 inclusion at school extend across the curriculum. For example, significant learning gains in mathematics are positively associated with bilingual teaching strategies; middle and high school students in dual-language programs are more likely to be enrolled in higher level math courses when compared to their peers in English-only programs (Lindholm-Leary & Borsato, 2005; Schüler-Meyer et al., 2019).

 "When school lessons are through the medium of Spanish, they do not solely feed a Spanish part of the brain. Or when other lessons are in English, they do not only feed the English part of the brain. Rather concepts learnt in one language can readily transfer into the other language." (Baker, 2011, p. 165)

A range of cognitive advantages are also associated with prolonged use and development of two languages. Bilinguals have been shown to have enhanced executive function (self-control, working memory, mental flexibility) and perform better in multitasking, paying attention, problem-solving, focusing, self-monitoring, and selecting relevant information than their monolingual peers (Bialystok et al., 2012; Marzecová et al., 2013). These cognitive benefits of bilingualism seen in children appear to persist across the lifespan (Bialystok et al., 2016; Kroll & Bialystok, 2013).

Assumption #2

Proficiency in the L1 is separate from proficiency in English.

Evidence: Most educational approaches to bilingualism and the learning of English are based on the assumption that proficiency in the L1 is separate from proficiency in the additional language (L2). If languages are distinct from one another and have no underlying proficiency that links them, it seems reasonable to argue that proficiency in English cannot be effectively developed by instruction through the L1 or through a combination of the L1 and English. However, what is logical is not necessarily valid. In this case, the evidence convincingly tells us that languages are not, in fact, separate in the cognitive system but rather readily transfer and interact within a single unified linguistic system.

"The reality is that students are making cross-linguistic connections throughout the course of their learning ... so why not nurture this learning strategy and help students apply it more efficiently?" (Cummins, 2007a, p. 229)

Literacy-related concepts and skills are interdependent across languages. Although the surface aspects of two languages (e.g., pronunciation, fluency) are clearly separate, they share a common underlying proficiency that enables transferability between the knowledge, skills, and concepts of the L1 and L2 (Cummins, 1991a, 2005). The L1 shares language resources with the L2 and vice versa. Correspondingly, a student's language and literacy development in their L1 is a strong predictor of their language and literacy development in their L2. This explains why research consistently shows that instruction through a minority language is not detrimental to students' academic performance in the majority language despite significantly less classroom time in the majority language (Thomas & Collier, 2002, 2004; Valentino & Reardon, 2015). More cognitively demanding tasks, like literacy, problem-solving, and abstract thinking, involve knowledge and competencies that are common across languages, which means that students can use what they know in their L1 to support their learning in English. Time spent developing L1 language and literacy skills is advantageous for developing English language and literacy skills as well.

Do your classroom policies and instructional strategies reflect an understanding of languages as interdependent or as separate from one another in the cognitive system?

Assumption #3

Translation between L1 and English is detrimental to language and literacy development and should be avoided.

Evidence: Transfer between the L1 and L2 is often only acknowledged in terms of errors made in English that are viewed as the result of interference from the L1. Translation between the L1 and English or vice versa is seldom seen as beneficial for the development of both languages. However, when we view languages as part of one unified linguistic system inside the mind of a bilingual, we can use instructional strategies that take advantage of language transfer and help students to apply it in effective ways. Translation can be particularly useful in vocabulary acquisition, which is an essential part of language competence as it is a key component of proficiency in all four major language skill areas—reading, writing, speaking, and listening—as well as the learning of content material.

 Neuroscience affirms that the initial acquisition of new words in a foreign language depends on the association of these items with corresponding L1 items in the learner's memory. (Sousa & Tomlinson, 2011)

For students with more advanced proficiency, English-only dictionaries and guessing meaning from context are useful strategies. For others, relying on these two methods alone is likely to cause frustration and waste valuable time and effort that could be better spent on more pedagogically beneficial tasks. Students with lower English proficiency often spend time looking up additional unknown words in the definition and struggle to execute higher order processes, like interpretation and inference, in English-only contexts. In such cases, direct word-to-word, L1–L2 translation is helpful. Students are more likely to gain a complete understanding of the word in a much shorter time.

If we dismiss the potential for translation to serve as a learning tool, we disregard substantial research that points to its value in L2 vocabulary acquisition. When used alongside other learning strategies, translation can play a key role in tapping into students' existing knowledge and cultivating metalinguistic awareness.

Assumption #4

Once students can speak English with reasonable fluency, they are ready to meet the demands of the curriculum solely in English.

Evidence: Students who are labeled as ELs or limited English proficient are sometimes prematurely reclassified as fluent English proficient as soon as they appear adept at conversational English. Conversational ability in an additional language can create a false impression that a student is ready to be taught exclusively through that language. Such students frequently fail to keep up in the classroom. As language supports are withdrawn, these students have difficulty understanding the content of the curriculum and struggle to engage in more cognitively demanding higher order classroom tasks (e.g., analysis, synthesis, evaluation, generalization, classification).

The distinction between academic language (used in school textbooks, informational texts, lectures, and scholarly papers) and social language (conversations composed of frequently heard vocabulary and speech patterns) is important for teachers to recognize to avoid the assumption that simply being immersed in an English-language environment and interacting with native speakers through cooperative learning structures will suffice for language development (Harper & Platt, 1998).

The development of academic language proficiency for ELs is a gradual and lengthy process made even more challenging because they are trying to catch up to their same-age native-English-speaking peers whose own academic language and literacy skills are continually progressing. L1 is a resource that many students greatly need to access curricular content, develop academic English language and skills, and engage in classroom-based cognitive processes more effectively. Remember, students who are developing literacy skills in their L1 are not just developing literacy skills in their L1; they are developing cognitive and linguistic competences that will transfer to academic English language and literacy competences and overall intellectual growth. Access to L1 creates pathways for ELs to engage with academic texts and effectively grapple with the lexical and grammatical structures used to convey increasingly complex concepts and information. Without these opportunities, there is little chance that they will be able to succeed at school.

Five Types of Cross-Lingual Transfer

According to Cummins (2005), there are five major types of cross-lingual transfer that will operate to varying degrees, depending on how conducive the sociolinguistic and educational situation is to such transfer. This is where we, as educators, come in. Being aware of the kinds of knowledge and learning strategies that can flow across languages helps us to integrate L1 in ways that more accurately reflect how our ELs are utilizing the languages in their toolkit. In principle, what this means for teaching ELs is that learning happens best when teachers explicitly draw students' attention to the differences and similarities between their languages and reinforce effective learning strategies in a coordinated way across languages (Cummins, 2007a). In practice, English-only instruction means this rarely, if ever, happens.

1. *Transfer of conceptual elements*: Conceptual knowledge in the L1 and L2 are interdependent. For example, a student who understands the concept of photosynthesis in their L1 means they need only learn the label (word) for that concept in the L2—a much lighter load, cognitively, than having to learn the label and the meaning simultaneously.

2. *Transfer of metacognitive and metalinguistic strategies*: Awareness of different language features and how they are used, strategies of visualizing, use of graphic organizers, mnemonic devices, vocabulary acquisition strategies.

3. *Transfer of pragmatic aspects of language use*: Willingness to take risks in communication through L2, ability to use nonverbal features, such as gestures or facial expressions, to aid communication.

4. *Transfer of specific linguistic elements*: Cognate connections—knowledge of the meaning of "photo" in photosynthesis.

5. *Transfer of phonological awareness*: The knowledge that words are composed of distinct sounds.

(Cummins, 2008)

Using Cummins's five types of cross-lingual transfer, brainstorm five instructional strategies and/or activities you could use in your classroom to take advantage of each (one strategy/activity for each type of transfer).

Teaching for Cross-Lingual Transfer

⭐ *Cocreate Multilingual Resources for Classroom Use* **(All levels)**
Although it is easy to tell teachers to make sure they stock their classrooms with a variety of age-appropriate, dual-language learning materials to promote language transfer, the reality is that finding resources that represent all the L1s in a linguistically diverse classroom can be difficult. One solution is to enlist the help of your students in creating them. Not only will teachers build up a stock of bilingual resources in multiple languages, but students will benefit from making cross-language connections and feel pride in creating educational materials for use in the classroom and/or school library. The Bangla/English bilingual poster example shown in Figure 1, complete with cards that can be flipped to reveal L1/L2 equivalencies, demonstrates what's possible.

These resources can be created across grade levels and subject areas. For example, a Grade 10 science class could create a bilingual diagram of photosynthesis, L1-diverse Grade 6 students could collaborate to make a multilingual poster of an ecosystem, or a

Figure 1. Bangla/English bilingual poster example. From "Jason Anderson: Teacher educator, author, consultant and researcher," by J. Anderson, n.d., www.jasonanderson.org.uk. Copyright 2017 by Jason Anderson. Reprinted with permission.

Grade 2 class could create bilingual children's books on geometry. There are countless possibilities that can be tailored to specific units of study in a variety of subjects. This activity is suitable for both English as a second language (ESL) and mixed student groups (i.e., ELs and native English speakers). An EL and a non-EL can work together to create bilingual materials, or groups of ESL students can create them on their own or with the help of a digital translation tool.

Translation as a Learning Tool

Student-Created Bilingual Dictionaries **(Grades 2–12, adult)**
Have ELs keep track of key words or phrases they learn in English by creating their own bilingual dictionaries or glossaries. Vocabulary can be recorded in notebooks or on mobile devices. Encourage students to complement one-word translations with example sentences. Younger students can create bilingual picture dictionaries by adding pictures or drawings to their vocabulary (see Madiha's example in Figure 2). These can be shared among students and serve as useful resources for teachers who can save copies for future classes. Introduce students to online bilingual dictionaries like www.WordReference.com or www.Linguee.com (also available as apps on iPhone or Android) which provide more context than machine translation tools.

Madiha, an EL in a Grade 7/8 classroom, illustrates how she draws from her L1 concepts and literacy to learn new vocabulary in English. Not restricted by monolingual instructional strategies that deny her access to her L1 as a resource for learning, Madiha is able to use both her L1 (Urdu) and her L2 (English) to learn and reinforce knowledge and strategies across languages.

The creation of bilingual dictionaries is suitable for mixed student groups and ESL classrooms. In mixed student classrooms, all students (not just the ELs) can be encouraged to investigate linguistic diversity, including the dialects of various cultural groups. Most native speakers of English—of all ethnicities—use different language registers (i.e., levels of formality) and codes (i.e., language forms) in different situations (Frederickson & Cline, 2009). Monolingual English speakers can work together to

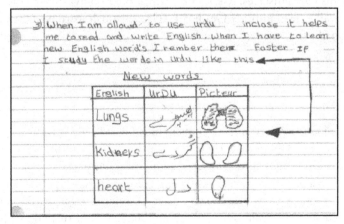

Figure 2. Madiha's illustration of strategies for learning English. From "Rethinking Monolingual Instructional Strategies in Multilingual Classrooms," by J. Cummins, 2007, *Canadian Journal of Applied Linguistics, 10*(2), pp. 221-240. Reprinted with permission. See also Bismilla (2006).

create bidialectal dictionaries in which they identify similarities and differences in their own vernacular versus other forms of English (e.g., in school texts) or slang versus formal language. It is useful for all students, regardless of language background, to examine how one form of language is legitimate and powerful in a particular context (e.g., among peer groups) while another form of language is necessary in a different context of use (e.g., at school).

Delayed Reverse Translations (Grades 3–12, adult)

Students translate an excerpt in English into their L1 on a separate piece of paper. The length or complexity of the passage is tailored to the students' proficiency level. Collect their work when they have finished. In a later lesson (e.g., the next day or following week), return students' L1 version of the text and ask them to translate it back into English. When the student finishes, return the original text, and have them compare their L1-to-English translation with the original excerpt in English. Put a few examples of students' translations on the board. Talk about how the two English versions are similar or different. Discuss words or phrases that were challenging and come up with strategies to help mitigate those difficulties in the future (e.g., idiomatic expressions, challenging grammatical structures).

This activity works best in ESL classrooms, but it can be used in mixed student groups as well. In mixed groups, have ELs complete the exercise using an excerpt from a classroom text that is being used in class by all students. When other students are engaging in individual or group work, have the ELs in the class share their translations with you or with other ELs. In this way, they are not only breaking down the linguistic components of the text, but also acquiring a better understanding of the content.

Multilingual Word Walls (All levels)

Although word walls are most common in primary grades (featuring high-frequency words that children are learning to read and write), they have a place in upper elementary, secondary, postsecondary, and ESL classrooms, too. Be sure to include short phrases as well as words on your wall—phrases are more meaningful than vocabulary items by themselves. Ask ELs to help add L1 equivalents to the English words on the wall. For example, a Grade 5 English/Spanish word wall created during a science unit on electricity might include

- atom / *átomo*
- electromagnetic force / *la fuerza electromagnética*
- potential energy / *la energía potencial*

This activity links vocabulary and concepts in meaningful ways across languages. It also elevates students' L1s to their rightful place alongside English. Secondary level classroom word walls can feature subject-specific vocabulary (e.g., math or science word walls) or relate to a particular unit of study (e.g., global citizenship, media literacy). In an ESL classroom, word walls can serve as visual reference for words related to a specific theme (e.g., food, technology, health and medicine) or related to a particular skill area (e.g., conjunctions in writing). Whatever the context or focus, word walls are dynamic and coconstructed. They are "living documents" that should be continually updated and interacted with as new vocabulary is introduced. This activity works well in both ESL and mixed student groups. Learning vocabulary across various languages increases metalinguistic awareness for everyone in the classroom, regardless of language background.

Examining Assumptions for Professional Development

Use the knowledge presented in this section to reflect on your own perceptions and practices related to ELs. Think about whether your planning and delivery of lessons takes advantage of cross-lingual transfer. If you don't already, commit to experimenting with flexible language pedagogies that recognize and harness students' L1 to support them in gaining access to the curriculum and engaging with complex texts.

Table 1 presents a summary of assumptions related to the education of ELs paired with the best knowledge we have based on current research. By reflecting on the misconceptions in the left column and embracing the knowledge in the right column, teachers can orchestrate more effective instruction by using students' L1 as a stepping stone to English language and content learning.

Table 1. Assumptions and Evidence About Teaching and Learning English Language and Content

Assumptions	Evidence
You learn English by using it, so any time that is spent using the L1 is time that could have been better spent practicing English.	The use of L1 (especially at early emergent levels) may save time, improve understanding, and build confidence in learners. It may even result in greater amounts of English being spoken.
Being immersed in an English-only environment is the fastest and most effective way to learn English.	The ability to explicitly draw on the knowledge and skills already developed in the L1 can result in efficiencies for learning academic English language and skills (e.g., learning strategies, cognate connections, and conceptual knowledge in the L1 can be transferred to English).
Languages are best learned in a natural way, in the same way that children learn their L1, without recourse to another language and without other languages getting in the way.	All learning is built upon what we already know, and learners will invariably make cross-lingual connections, whether we like it or not. Furthermore, L1 acquisition is very different from the learning of another language later in life. The absence of an L1 is a situation that can never be replicated among school-aged children and youth.
Learners need to learn English through English so that they do not make mistakes that are caused by L1 interference.	Research suggests that ELs learn best when teachers explicitly draw attention to the similarities and differences between their languages and build upon effective learning strategies in a synchronized way across languages.
Translation is detrimental to language learning.	Translation is one of the most natural and frequent activities in real-life situations where two languages are involved. It can be used strategically to support students in making connections between their L1 and English. Moreover, it is a valuable skill in our diverse global society.

(continued on the next page)

Table 1. *(continued)*

Assumptions	Evidence
When an EL uses their L1 in class or translanguages (uses their full language repertoire in the course of a single conversation) they are being careless or they are compensating for an inability to speak and understand English.	The language practices students engage in are often strategic and purposeful. ELs make language choices in response to context and audience or a desire to identify with a particular group. It is wrong to assume that L1 use is always the result of an incomplete knowledge of English.
Once students can converse easily with teachers and classmates, they are ready to learn solely through English.	Fluency in conversational English does not mean students have developed sufficient academic English to cope with the curriculum exclusively in English. Academic language is primarily found in texts and course materials, so it is crucial that students have abundant access to literacy materials in both L1 and English.
Students cannot work with grade-level content until they develop English language proficiency.	When students have explicit access to their L1 and all of the prior knowledge encoded within, they can engage with age-appropriate curricular content *without waiting*. This means that as they learn English, they do not fall progressively behind in the curriculum.
Good teaching is good enough for everyone, including ELs.	Though ELs may benefit from aspects of good instruction, teachers need to have sufficient background knowledge on additional language acquisition and the benefits of biliteracy education. Instruction should include the use of students' L1 and a focus on academic language development. Students' unique knowledge and skills should be extended and connected to the curriculum—one size does not fit all.
Parents or caregivers of ELs do not want to be involved in their children's school-based education.	Parents of ELs may not feel that what happens at home is valued in their child's school setting. They may share many of the same assumptions that educators do and feel an English-only environment is best. There may also be language barriers that contribute to exclusion. It is crucial for teachers to have an ongoing, open dialogue with families. Involve families in their child's schooling through use of the L1 and communicate to caregivers that developing L1 language and literacy helps develop school-based language and literacy as well.
Monolingual teachers have no choice but to use English as the exclusive language of instruction.	You do not have to be bilingual to implement bilingual instructional strategies. Providing spaces where students can draw on their full linguistic repertoire for learning purposes can be accomplished individually (e.g., with the help of an online translation tool or activities like brainstorming in the L1) or in same-L1 pairs or groups (e.g., to discuss a complex text).

Note: EL = English learner, L1 = home language.

This table can be distributed as a handout and/or used as an icebreaker in a professional development workshop or a preservice teacher education class. Cut out the assumption statements in the left column and distribute one to each attendee (there will be multiples). Do not tell them that these are "assumptions"; use them as talking points to introduce the session or lesson. Have participants find a partner, read their statements to each other, and discuss whether they agree or disagree with each and why. After a few minutes of discussion time, have pairs exchange sentence strips and find a new partner until everyone has had a chance to discuss each statement. At the end of the information session, encourage critical reflection by asking participants to think about the conversations they had during the icebreaker at the beginning. What did they learn? Have any of their original opinions changed?

Another option is to distribute one statement to each participant and have them work together to reconstruct the table by identifying the assumptions and their corresponding evidence. Provide Table 1 as a handout or project it on the screen to discuss as a whole group to consolidate the professional development or preservice training.

Beyond breaking down some of our assumptions about teaching and learning English language and content, L1 plays a vital role in affirming students' developing identities and creating more inclusive learning environments. Next, we look at the role of L1 in student identity formation and in promoting more equitable educational opportunities for ELs.

The Role of Home Language in Student Identity Formation

It is critically important for teachers to recognize that a child's language is inextricably interwoven with their family, community, and personal identity. To suggest that this language is "wrong" by discouraging its use is to suggest that something is wrong with the student and their loved ones. To suggest that this language is not useful at school by designating the classroom an English-only zone is to disregard an integral part of who a student is and imply that part is irrelevant to what they do at school.

 Grade 7/8 teacher, Lisa Leoni, discusses the importance of student identity in informing her instructional choices: "The way I see it everything has to relate to the identity of the students; children have to see themselves in every aspect of their work at school. My overarching goal as a teacher is to uncover all that is unknown to me about my students—linguistically and culturally, and especially to understand the community they are part of (their parents, their friends, their faith) and the list goes on. So, when a student enters my class, I want to discover all that I can about that student as a learner and as a person. For example, when Tomer entered my class last year, a lot of the work he produced was in Hebrew. Why? Because that is where his knowledge was encoded, and I wanted to make sure that Tomer was an active member and participant in my class. It was also a way for me to gain insight into his level of literacy and oral language development." (as cited in Cummins, 2007b, p. 1)

There is general consensus in education that connecting learning to students' interests, experiences, and prior knowledge is key to making it meaningful and engaging. For many ELs, that prior knowledge and experience is encoded in their L1. Negative messages, intentional or not, are sent to a student about their identity when they are asked to leave their L1 at the classroom door. Language is not neutral. It is not simply an abstract code that we use to think and communicate. It is fundamental to a person's personal and collective identity (Cummins, 2000b).

 "The starting point for understanding why students choose to engage academically or, alternatively, withdraw from academic effort is to acknowledge that *human relationships are at the heart of schooling.* All of us intuitively know this from our own schooling experiences. If we felt that a teacher believed in us and cared for us then we put forth much more effort than if we felt that she or he did not like us or considered us not very capable." (Cummins, 2000a, p. 40)

When students' identities are affirmed by instruction that validates their languages, culture, and experiences by utilizing them as linguistic and intellectual resources, connections are made between the curriculum and students' lives; learning becomes more meaningful and productive. Students participate more actively and put in more effort. They learn more and experience better academic outcomes. The more students learn and achieve, they more they want to learn and achieve, and the more they are willing to invest in learning.

Alternatively, when students' identities are devalued through policies or instruction that excludes their language, culture, and experiences, there is little opportunity for meaningful connection between their lives and the curriculum. They are expected to learn in an environment detached from who they are and what they know. The result is often withdrawal. Silence and lack of participation are then frequently interpreted by teachers as an inability to cope with the curriculum and/or a lack of effort. Teachers lower their expectations, and students internalize this perceived failure. Those low expectations become self-fulfilling.

To disrupt patterns of underachievement, teachers must choose instructional strategies that validate culturally and linguistically diverse students' prior knowledge and experience (much of which is encoded in their L1)—instruction that enables students to develop and enact what Manyak (2004) described as "identities of competence" related to literacy and overall academic growth. These teacher-student interactions constitute the most immediate determinant of student academic success or failure (Cummins, 1997).

 "When students are treated as competent they are likely to demonstrate competence." (Ladson-Billings, 1994, p. 123)

Step 1: What is your personal teacher identity? Free-write for 10 minutes on how you define your role as an educator of culturally and linguistically diverse students. What do you expect of yourself and your students? What are your intentions, assumptions, and goals?

Step 2: Read what you wrote and think about how the various expectations, assumptions, and goals you bring to the task of educating these students shapes your interactions with them. Reflect on ways your teacher identity might act to either constrict or extend your students' identities and learning.

See Appendix B for a Personal Teacher Identity Reflection Tool.

Identity Self-Portraits

Teachers cannot incorporate students' languages, cultures, or experiences into the classroom unless they know what they are. There are activities that can be done at the beginning of the school year to facilitate this, such as language maps or biographies or identity self-portraits. These projects are versatile and can be adapted to any grade level. Teachers can choose how structured or unstructured they want the process to be, although it should be flexible enough to elicit various approaches, permit students to be creative, and invest their identity in the product.

Cultural and Linguistic Self-Portraits (Grades K–6)

Prasad (2015) worked with students in Grades 4 to 6 in Canada and France to create plurilingual, multimodal texts, including cultural and linguistic self-portraits using paper collages as a background. To see samples of student work and more about the project, visit: I am plurilingual! Je suis plurilingue! (www.iamplurilingual.com).

Prasad (2015) describes the activity as follows: Begin by having students associate a color with each language or culture they consider to be a part of their lives, then tear or cut pieces of colored paper to represent proportionally their relationship to each language or culture (e.g., a student might use more of one color to illustrate that they feel a stronger attachment to the corresponding language, or less of a color to show limited use of that language in their daily life).

After completing their paper collage background, have students cut out a personal black and white digital photograph of themselves generated in photo-editing software. This body outline will serve as map on which they locate the different languages and cultures that play a role in their life. Students can make choices about which colors they use to represent each language, as well as where they place each language or culture on their body. In the process of making these creative representational pieces, encourage students to reflect about the languages and cultures in their lives. Ask students to use color and embodied metaphors to describe their feelings about, use of, and relationship with each language and culture in their communicative repertoire. View these self-portraits at www.iamplurilingual.com/self-portraits.html.

Remix: Mixed-Media Identity Self-Portraits (Grades 7–12, adult)

This assignment, created by Hassapopoulou (2013), involves remixing and appropriating found digital objects. Though it was designed for a university-level English composition class, this project is suitable for younger students, as well—requirements and assessment standards can be adapted accordingly, as well as the final presentation. Hassapopoulou (2013) provides the following assignment guidelines to students:

> Find and analyze one video and one picture/image from the internet that each represents part of your identity and/or that you identify with. Explain why/if these objects fully represent what you wanted to find online, and how you—as a producer—would modify and customize them to adequately encapsulate your [identity].
>
> *Objective*: Reflect on the process of selection: the internet is a vast (and sometimes chaotic) archive; how did you narrow your selection down to these 2 specific digital objects? In this assignment, you are challenged to apply persuasive reasoning to justify why and how your media represent facets of your identity. You are essentially trying to write (yourself) through media, and to find personal meaning in existing sources. (para. 4–5)

Students are asked to post their found media and analysis (of approximately 1,000 words) to their blog and cite all their sources. On the day the assignment is due, students give a brief presentation of their blog essay to the class.

For more details on this assignment and samples of student work, visit jitp.commons.gc.cuny.edu/authentic-hybridity-remix-and-appropriation-as-multimodal-composition.

Teaching for Cross-Lingual Transfer

Identity Texts (Grades 3–12, adult)

Pioneered by ESL teacher Patricia Chow (Chow & Cummins, 2003), identity texts are creative, multimodal projects in which students invest and express their identity. Sharing identity texts (e.g., through technology) with multiple audiences (e.g., family, friends, the wider school population, the media) often results in positive feedback that contributes to a student's affirmation of self (Cummins & Early, 2011). Dual-language identity texts encourage students to express themselves through both of their languages in the context of a cognitively demanding task. These projects enable ELs to see themselves as academically competent bilinguals, which fuels academic engagement.

Because identity texts generally require considerable time to complete, it is useful to make cross-curricular connections so that they meet standards in several different content areas. For example, students could document the life of an older individual in their family or community by researching the historical context in which the individual grew up, conducting interviews, and creating a dual-language digital text. This project would integrate curricular objectives in social studies, language arts, and technology.

The teacher can provide the frame within which the identity text is created and offer suggestions, but students should be free to choose a topic that is relevant to them and decide how they will carry it out (e.g., creative writing, art, drama, video production). It is essential that these projects are student-led so that students *want* to invest in them and feel ownership over the process and product.

For an overview of identity text projects including samples of student work, see Cummins et al. (2005). Visit identity text projects and exhibitions online to get inspired:

- The Dual-Language Showcase
  (schools.peelschools.org/1363/DualLanguage/Documents/index2.htm)

- Family Treasures and Grandma's Soup: A Dual Language Book Project
  (www.duallanguageproject.com/index.html)

- Floradale Elementary School: Infusing Dual Language Literacy Through the Library Curriculum (www.multiliteracies.ca/index.php/folio/viewProject/5)

- Sister-Class Project: Toronto & Hong Kong
  (www.multiliteracies.ca/index.php/folio/viewProject/51)

- Songide'ewin: Aboriginal Narratives
  (www.youtube.com/watch?v=Tk5tTtVM2jQ)

Grade 7 student Kanta Khalid describes her experience cocreating the dual-language Urdu-English identity text, *The New Country*, with two same-L1 peers: "How it helped me was when I came here in Grade 4 the teachers didn't know what I was capable of. I was given a pack of crayons and a coloring book and told to get on coloring with it. And after I felt so bad about that—I'm capable of doing much more than just that. I have my own inner skills to show the world than just coloring and I felt that those skills of mine are important also. So when we started writing the book [*The New Country*], I could actually show the world that I am something instead of just coloring. And that's how it helped me and it made me so proud of myself that I am actually capable of doing something . . . I'm not just a coloring person—I can show you that I am something." (Cummins & Early, 2011, p. 50)

Identities are not singular or static. They change over time and within different contexts and situations; they are multiple and complex, and culturally based. The relationship that is formed between a student and teacher is a process of *identity negotiation*, "represented by the messages communicated to students regarding their identities— who they are in the teacher's eyes and who they are capable of becoming" (Cummins, 2000b, p. 166). Teacher identity—how a teacher defines their role in the context of broader societal and educational structures— influences how they interact with students from diverse cultural and linguistic backgrounds. These interactions are consequential in determining students' engagement in learning and, ultimately, their success at school. As Cummins and Early (2011) point out,

> educators have considerable power to affect student identity construction in positive (and, unfortunately, in negative) ways. Teachers' instructional choices within the classroom play a huge role in

determining the extent to which students will emerge from an identity cocoon defined by their assumed limitations (e.g., the "ESL student") to an interpersonal space defined by their talents and accomplishment, both linguistic and intellectual. For this to happen, teachers must "see through" the institutional labels to the potential within. (p. xvi)

Using Home Language to Advance Social Justice in the Classroom

Explanations of underachievement in ELs are various and complex, but many are based on the assumptions discussed earlier in this chapter. Bilingualism itself is often assigned blame for its perceived role in causing cognitive confusion. However, research shows that when students are provided with the educational support to sufficiently develop both languages, bilingualism is likely to produce cognitive advantages, not disadvantages.

Lack of exposure to English is also a typical explanation for the underachievement of language minoritized students,[1] so transitional bilingual programs aim to achieve a fast conversion to mainstream classrooms where English is the sole medium of instruction. But because mainstream and subject specialist teachers still predominantly maintain their classrooms as English-only zones, students are denied access to their L1, denied the cognitive and academic competencies already available through that L1, and frequently denied their identity and self-esteem.

As Delpit and Dowdy (2002) argue, it is not "children's language that causes educational problems, but the educational bureaucracy's response to the language" (p. xxi). The persistent achievement gap between ELs and non-ELs is not because children from the latter group are inherently smarter; they are advantaged because curriculum and assessment standards are "patterned, normed, and created for them" (Pérez & Saavedra, 2017, p. 11).

Socially just instruction for ELs begins with recognizing the ways in which language can serve to either empower or marginalize. Schools in the United States, Canada, and other westernized countries often operate with "a narrow monolingual, monocultural model of what it means to be 'literate'" (Grant & Wong, 2008, p. 166). This inevitably produces and perpetuates barriers to literacy for culturally and linguistically diverse children and youth as well as those from low socioeconomic backgrounds. The illusion of an equal educational system (i.e., education is available equally to all) is propped up by curriculum reform policy, teaching practices, and high-stakes testing measures that sustain singular, Eurocentric, and English-only conceptions of literacy (Grant & Wong, 2008).

ELs, particularly refugees or those from lower socioeconomic backgrounds who experience academic difficulties, are often subject to lower expectations and consequently held up to less rigorous standards than their middle-to-upper-class native-English-speaking counterparts. We know that low expectations significantly affect

---

[1] I use the term *minoritized* to signal the societal power relations inherent in such labels. Bishop (2013) notes that to be designated a minority, "one does not need to be in the numerical minority but only treated as if one's position and perspective are of less worth; to be silenced or marginalized" (p. 74).

academic achievement (Rubie-Davies, 2008; Tavani & Losh, 2003). Studies show that minoritized students and students from low-income families seem to be disproportionately affected by negatively biased teacher expectations (Hinnant et al., 2009; Sorhagen, 2013). The expectations teachers hold affect how they behave toward students and those interactions affect students' identity and academic outcomes. Teachers who have lower expectations for students provide fewer opportunities to learn for these students; high-expectation students are generally provided with more chances to respond, more challenging instruction, more praise, and more supportive and caring interactions (de Boer et al., 2018).

This is actualized in schools when an EL child is handed yet another worksheet while her classmates write stories or engage in dramatic play, or when a refugee youth who is regularly left out of cognitively challenging work fails another standardized test and concludes that he is "just no good at school." These are invariably perceived as individual failings and not problematized as symptoms of low expectations and broader structural inequities. It is crucial for educators to examine their own teacher expectation biases. It is only by naming and disrupting structural inequities and orchestrating instruction that actively includes those who have historically been excluded from education that we provide truly equitable educational environments.

 "Inclusion is not bringing people into what already exists; it is making a new space, a better space for everyone." (Dei, 2016, p. 36)

 Think about a high-performing student and a low-performing student you have or have had in the past. If you are a preservice teacher, consider asking a practicing teacher these questions, or think about experiences you have had in your student teaching:

- Where did your expectations for each student come from (e.g., discussions with the students' previous teachers; classroom behavior; biases you may have about their race, class, language background)?

- How did your expectations and underlying beliefs affect your interactions with those students?

- Did you give them equal opportunities to learn and demonstrate learning?

- If not, how could you have done better?

Developing Critical Language Awareness

Although proficiency in cognitive academic language is necessary for students to be able to cope with the demands of the curriculum, we must recognize that school-based language and literacy practices do not represent the only or "best" way of speaking, doing, and being. Rather, they are one specific context for complex language production and meaning making. Developing a critical language awareness means that students are involved in conversations that critically examine how language is connected to larger constructs of power and inequality. Students should understand that there is nothing that makes academic language intrinsically better than other language varieties but, at the same time, they should be supported in developing an awareness that language choices are not neutral. As teachers, we can help them learn when to suppress and select features from their linguistic repertoire appropriately for different purposes in different contexts. All students are entitled to education that develops and maintains their own language and language varieties *and also* gives them access to academic language, widely seen as the language of economic success.

"I suggest that students must be taught the codes needed to participate fully in the mainstream of American life, not by being forced to attend to hollow, inane, decontextualized subskills, but rather within the context of meaningful communicative endeavors; that they must be allowed the resource of the teacher's expert knowledge, while being helped to acknowledge their own 'expertness' as well; and that even while students are assisted in learning the culture of power, they must also be helped to learn about the arbitrariness of those codes and about the power relationships they represent." (Delpit, 1988, p. 296)

Developing a Critical Language Awareness in Young Children (Grades K–6)

Even very young children are capable of engaging in critical dialogue on sensitive and controversial topics (Souto-Manning, 2013; Vasquez, 2014). Critical language awareness involves unpacking the relationship between language and power—figuring out how systems work to position people inequitably based on language practices. The strategies you choose to engage students in for developing this critical frame depends on your knowing your students and observing them closely. Opportunities to engage in critical language awareness arise when spaces are created for children to give voice to what they notice around them and how that relates to their lived experiences.

In a Grade 1 classroom with several Korean-L1 students, for example, the teacher might involve children in conversations about the similarities and differences between English and Korean. The Korean students can teach the teacher and their classmates aspects of their L1 (e.g., vocabulary, simple phrases), and the class can compare those with English equivalences. The Korean students experience validation and pride in being able to exchange knowledge and skills with classmates, and monolingual English children develop an appreciation for a language other than English. Teachers can guide discussion about how although Korean and English are different, one is not better than the other.

Teachers might also have their students become "language detectives" by watching and listening to a variety of video and audio and examining the differences and similarities in how people talk. Children learn that there are many different ways to say the same thing and that different languages and ways of speaking are appropriate in different situations and with different people.

Role-plays are another excellent way of having students practice English in a way that does not revere it as the only correct way of speaking. Students can memorize and perform reading scripts from grade-level books or stories, which gives them a chance to practice English without worrying about being corrected. They can create puppet shows or role-play popular cartoon characters or superheroes. As Delpit (2006) points out, many superheroes speak almost hypercorrect Standard English. Playing a role gives a child a chance to practice language in a nonthreatening way, one that does not imply that their own language or language variety is inadequate but rather suggests that different language performances are appropriate in different contexts.

⭐ *Developing a Critical Language Awareness in Older Children* (Grades 6–12, adult)

In upper elementary and secondary grades as well as in adult education, teachers may opt to initiate discussions of language, identity, and power by examining stereotypes (e.g., have students compare media portrayals of their language and culture to their own lived realities during a media literacy unit) or by listening to and reading different language varieties and considering how those styles impact the message and different audiences (e.g., a teacher, an older individual in the community, a peer group). Additionally, discussion questions like those following can be adapted by teachers to reflect the grade level, context (e.g., ESL vs. mixed student group), or curricular frame (e.g., connecting it to a particular unit of study, like global citizenship). Questions like these encourage students to critically reflect on language, explore the relationship between language and identity, and deconstruct assumptions about what it means to be bilingual or to use languages or English dialects outside of what is expected at school.

Questions for Critical Language Awareness

- In what ways are the languages you speak connected to your identity?

- What is the difference between your language and your nationality?

- What is a native speaker? Are you a native speaker of a language?

- Does your language give you a sense of belonging to a certain group?

- Has your language ever made you feel like an "outsider"?

- What are some stereotypes associated with different language groups?

- What languages are powerful?

- What languages are marginalized?

- In what ways can being bilingual give you power?

Students can respond with written reflections or in discussion groups. Encourage ELs to discuss or write using their L1 and share with the class in English. Projects or in-class presentations could also be designed around one or several of these questions.

Equalizing power relations in the classroom means that the teacher is not the only expert, but rather shares their expertise with the students who sometimes know more than they do, for example, about their languages or culture. When students are able to invest their identity into the creation of classroom products, project that identity into social spaces, and receive positive feedback, they feel pride and ownership over their learning and experience positive identity affirmation (Cummins & Early, 2011). Lessons like those included here create opportunities to do this.

Incorporating students' L1 into classroom learning does not require an overhaul of your existing repository of lesson plans. You can extend or modify activities you already use, like I have done to the following lessons. These modifications and extensions create spaces for students to make connections between prior and new knowledge and feel pride in what they know and are learning.

Amplifying Diverse Voices: A Collection of Lesson Plans

The following lessons incorporate interrelated strands of a history curriculum and require students to use their linguistic repertoires to study English and history in authentic ways. Short summaries of lessons and links to full plans and materials are included in each lesson, along with descriptions of how to extend or modify these lessons to enhance learning for *all* students in the classroom.

Varying Views of America (Grades 9–12)
After review of the literary elements of tone and point of view, students work together to read, summarize, and reflect on three poems about America written from diverse perspectives. This sample lesson plan uses Walt Whitman's "I Hear America Singing," Langston Hughes's "I, Too, Sing America," and Maya Angelou's "On the Pulse of the Morning."

Link to Full Lesson and Materials: www.readwritethink.org/classroom-resources/lesson-plans/varying-views-america-194.html (Lesson Author: Sharon Webster, Narragansett, Rhode Island)

Modification: Allow ELs to use their L1 in same-L1 peer groups to discuss, annotate, and summarize the three poems. You can substitute or add poems written by people from the same background as your ELs, including bilingual poems (e.g., "Betting on America" by Richard Blanco) or poems written in languages other than English (e.g., "Sustancia" by Julio Marzán).

Extension: Students create their own poems using tone and point of view to express how they see and experience America using English, L1, or both. These activities culminate in a poetry slam where students perform their poems in their chosen language(s) and mode (e.g., music, video, drama, oral recitation). Use technology to amplify their work by reaching wider audiences by, for example, uploading students' poems and/or performances to a class or school website.

They're Coming to America: Immigrants Past and Present (Grades 6–12)
Students explore historic waves of immigration, key motivations for immigration, and compare and contrast contemporary and historic immigrant experiences in America.

Link to Full Lesson and Materials: www.pbslearningmedia.org/resource/foa10.soc.K-6.histus.lpcoming/theyre-coming-to-america-immigrants-past-and-present

Modification/Extension: Engage students in a critical discussion of the statement: "America is a nation of immigrants." Encourage students to think about the cultural assumptions underlying the statement and problematize the terms *migrate* and *Land of Opportunity*.

Through which cultural lens do we assume that all of those who landed on American soil were migrants looking for a better life? If needed, prompt students by asking who is being excluded in the "nation of immigrants" narrative (i.e., Indigenous peoples; those who were enslaved and brought to America in chains). The idealized American immigrant story typically leaves out Indigenous and Black experiences and masks settler colonialism, slavery, and systemic inequities. Emphasize the importance of identifying the dominant narrative and looking outside of it. This discussion might lead into a lesson on settler colonialism or a history unit that covers the transatlantic slave trade, the experience of slavery in America from 1619 to the Civil War, Reconstruction, Jim Crow, and the civil rights era.

Extension: After several lessons on family history to scaffold the process, students collect information and formulate questions to interview family members. Students explore and discuss family histories and conduct interviews with family members in one or more languages. They use the compiled information to create (bilingual) audiovisual family history presentations that can be shared with school, family, and community members.

Proverbs: At Home and Around the World (Grades 4–8)

Students explore how proverbs are connected to cultural knowledge and values, as well as how proverbs from different cultures are similar and different. Students gather family proverbs with the help of parents or family/community members, share them with the class, and explain their significance. As a culminating project, students select one or two proverbs and use art materials, PowerPoint, or a word processor to create posters that can be displayed around the school or classroom.

Link to Full Lesson and Materials: www.readwritethink.org/classroom-resources/lesson-plans/proverbs-home-around-world-185.html (Lesson Author: John Paul Walter, Washington, DC)

Modification: Encourage ELs to find proverbs in their L1. This gives parents or caregivers who have limited English language or literacy skills the opportunity to get involved in their child's learning. Students and family members can work together to translate proverbs into English. In class, initiate discussion on what equivalencies were found between the L1 and English proverbs and what language or concepts were difficult to translate. Investigate whether there are similar English proverbs. (E.g., the Italian proverb *Chi dorme non piglia pesci*, translated as "He who sleeps doesn't catch any fish," might be an equivalent to the English proverb "The early bird gets the worm.") Talk about the meaning and cultural significance behind the proverbs. Encourage ELs to create bilingual posters.

Exploring Language and Identity: Amy Tan's "Mother Tongue" and Beyond (Grades 9–12)

Students explore the relationship between language and identity by reflecting on the different languages or "different Englishes" they use in speaking and writing, and when and where these languages are appropriate. Students read and discuss Amy Tan's essay, "Mother Tongue." Finally, students write a literacy narrative describing two different languages they use.

Link to Full Lesson and Materials: www.readwritethink.org/classroom-resources/lesson
-plans/exploring-language-identity-mother-910.html (Lesson Author: Renee H. Shea,
Rockville, Maryland)

Modification: Group same-L1 peers together so they can use their L1 to discuss Tan's
essay. Give students the choice of what language they write in.

Rather than doing a written literacy narrative, another option is to encourage
students to represent their languages pictorially using geographic maps, organizational
trees, pictures, streetscapes, lists, or aerial views and text in multiple languages. D'warte
(2014), who documented an activity like this in Grade 5 and 6 classrooms, noted that
the process engaged all students in rich discussion as they talked about how, when,
where, and why language changed in different contexts and for different audiences and
why these changes mattered in meaning making. Students can discuss their "language
maps" in groups, then present them to the class. To extend the activity further, have
students choose a context or interaction from their language maps to write a script for a
role-play.

 How would you reimagine a lesson or unit you teach through a social justice lens?
What modifications or extensions could you use that harness students' language
resources and prior knowledge (*the how*) to support them in meeting curriculum
standards (*the what*)?

For templates, see Appendix C (Plurilingual Lesson Planning Template) and Appendix D
(Plurilingual Unit Planning Template).

Make Language Diversity a Part of the Curriculum

We must find ways in our classrooms to celebrate and sustain diversity rather than
simply tolerate it. Make language diversity a part of your curriculum. Find opportunities
throughout the year to honor and explore students' own cultural and linguistic history.
Ask students to teach you and other students in the class aspects of their language or
language variety. To develop academic language in a way that does not make value
judgements (i.e., implying that a student's own language or language variety is inadequate), have students translate stories, songs, and poems in their L1 or own English
dialect into academic English (e.g., translate a hip-hop or K-pop song into academic
English using formal vocabulary and rhetorical conventions and changing syntactical
structures). Younger students can put on plays or puppet shows and role-play using
different languages and English dialects.

Extend the Curriculum (Grades 6–12, adult)
Begin the year by having students study their own cultural and linguistic
background (be it distant Irish ancestors or a country they have recently
emigrated from) including the history, resources, people, and so on. As the year
progresses and students learn aspects of the state curriculum, ask them to connect that
knowledge to relevant aspects of their ancestry and share those connections with the
class. The greater your knowledge of diverse cultures and their intellectual legacies, the
more you will be able to support students in making those connections.

This idea is suitable for both ESL and mixed student groups. In any context, activities that extend the curriculum to envelop diverse languages and cultures create opportunities for students to see themselves in what they are being taught. If we do not explicitly make these connections, we risk alienating diverse students with a curriculum that presents a narrative that does not fit into their experiences and histories. Moreover, sharing the history and contributions of other linguistic and cultural groups broadens the minds and enriches the learning environment for everyone.

 Stephanie Terry, a first-grade teacher at an inner-city school in Baltimore, Maryland with 100 percent African-American enrollment, tells her students about the world's first libraries, which were established in Africa, while covering a unit about libraries. During a unit on health, she describes to her class the African doctors of antiquity who wrote the first texts on medicine. Stephanie is not replacing the curriculum; she is expanding it in ways that connect it to her students' identities. She also teaches about the contributions of Asian-Americans, Native Americans, and Latinos. (For more, see Delpit, 2006, pp. 181–183)

Chapter 1 Review

Teachers have the transformational power to choose instructional strategies that do not implicitly devalue diverse students' language, culture, and identity. Until we recognize and learn about what Delpit (2006) describes as "the brilliance the students bring with them 'in their blood'" (p. 182), we will not appreciate their potential and we will struggle to connect the subject matter we teach to their lives and histories. Equipped with a greater understanding of how ELs' prior knowledge and rich and complex linguistic repertoires can be harnessed at school, we can more effectively support the development of academic skills, disrupt unjust educational structures, and cultivate more inclusive classrooms that produce more equitable academic outcomes for marginalized students.

Chapter 1 provided fundamental knowledge for the effective instruction of ELs. This chapter exposed common misconceptions about language learning and addressed why including L1 in classroom learning is essential to students' success at school and a vital part of promoting greater educational equity. Key points are summarized as follows:

- A large and growing body of research has established that the use of students' L1 in instruction promotes additional language learning, literacy development, and more effective acquisition of curricular content and skills.

- Languages in the mind readily interact and build upon one another, so the academic language and literacy skills that students develop to help them read and write in their L1 help them as they learn to read and write in English.

- L1 provides ELs with a vital language support for grappling with academic English and engaging in higher order thinking.

- Use of the L1 gives ELs access to the curriculum. They are able to develop content knowledge and skills irrespective of their English language proficiency. This means that as they learn English, they do not fall progressively further behind in the curriculum.

- Students' L1 is inextricable from their identity. When it is excluded from classroom learning, there is an implicit devaluation of who they are and what they bring to the classroom. Students need to see themselves in the work they do at school. For ELs, this is impossible to fully realize in an English-only environment.

- Power relations and broader structural inequities need to be recognized as key factors in educational underachievement among marginalized groups. A classroom that validates languages other than English pushes back against inequitable power relations in school and society and sends a clear message to students and parents: Your languages, cultures, and identities are legitimate and valued.

Chapter 1 provided the knowledge base for understanding why students' L1s are an indispensable part of providing more equitable educational opportunities for ELs.

CHAPTER 2

OUT OF MINDS AND INTO CLASSROOM SPACES: WHEN, HOW, AND HOW MUCH HOME LANGUAGE TO INCORPORATE INTO INSTRUCTION

Any classroom with students who speak languages other than English is multilingual. Whether those other languages are given legitimacy and voice in an officially monolingual classroom or remain confined inside the minds of bilingual students is another issue. Even among proponents of home language (L1) use, there are conflicting views on how and when it should be harnessed for learning purposes. Some favor a measured approach that utilizes L1 at specific times for specific purposes (Centeno-Cortés & Jiménez Jiménez, 2004). Others advocate for seeing the language classroom as a consistently "bilingual space" where students have unrestricted access to their full language repertoire (García, Johnson et al., 2017).

Without more definitive research on when L1 use in the classroom most optimally benefits learners, there is arguably no correct answer that can be applied universally. The best we can do is make informed decisions that consider context, targeted learning outcomes, and the individual students in our classroom in a given year. You may discover that a fully multilingual environment where English learners (ELs) can draw on all of their linguistic resources throughout the course of a day works best. Or you may feel that maintaining an official space for "English-only" is necessary to provide the appropriate opportunities for language development while allowing for some flexibility in students' language use for specific tasks.

Regardless of the context in which we teach, we all make instructional choices regarding how we deliver the curriculum and measure students' success in achieving objectives. The choices we make are not neutral. We must ask ourselves: What perspectives and beliefs underlie those choices? What learning are we attempting to produce and why? Teachers should think strategically about the purpose of a given activity or lesson.

Language develops through use and interaction, so English should be a priority in every classroom, but it should not be the only priority. ELs are also learning the content of the curriculum at the same time they are learning the language of instruction. To keep pace with same-age peers, they need to deeply understand the content they are learning. There will be times in the classroom when making connections to background knowledge, clarifying instructions or concepts, or affirming bilingual and biliterate identities will be of greater importance in that moment than practicing the use of academic English. There will also be times when the purpose of the writing or discussion is to explicitly practice the English language vocabulary and structures related to the topic.

Keep an open dialogue with students to help determine when and how much L1 to involve in learning. Including students in determining acceptable language practices in the classroom will increase the likelihood that they will follow those guidelines. Encourage students to share when a particular strategy works for them, take note of small and large breakthroughs (e.g., a student is more engaged, creates a project they are proud of, or connects a learning point to their real life), and use this information to inform instructional decisions.

 Why might you encourage L1 use? Have you ever encouraged students to use their L1 in the classroom? What benefits did you find? Do you have any concerns about allowing ELs to use their L1? Think of some ways that you could mitigate any perceived negative effects.

Structured Home Language Time

If you choose to forgo a more flexible classroom environment where students are permitted unrestricted access to their L1 for a more structured approach, you may need some tools to ensure that "L1 time" does not spill over into designated English-only time. Consider color-coding times on the daily agenda or using a signal or sign, like a flag or traffic light symbols (i.e., red light for English-only time, green for L1, and yellow to signal an intermediate period when students are free to draw on any language in their repertoire). A more structured approach does not have to mean a rigid approach. A signaling system can be used to experiment with what works best in your classroom. If you discover that the intermediate period where students can use a combination of their L1 and English is producing better results, then you and your students can choose to extend that time or eventually discard the system entirely in favor of a flexible languaging environment.

In any context, different students respond in different ways to particular instructional techniques and teacher-student relationships. Some students may prefer structured and predictable routines, others may be comfortable with more informal interactions and spontaneous learning activities. Some ELs may want to use their L1 in the classroom while others might be resistant to it. Tell your students why you are encouraging them to use their L1 in a particular circumstance or, alternatively, why you believe using English-only for a particular activity is better. Explain the reasons behind your choices in the classroom and encourage students, at any grade level, to communicate their needs. Cooperative decision-making—at the task level or for a more long-term unit of study or project—usually produces the best outcome. Ask a same-L1 peer, upper grade mentor, or bilingual colleague, or use an online translation tool to help facilitate these conversations. ELs are a richly heterogenous group—how you think someone will learn something is not always how they actually learn it. Work together with your students, experiment, and discover collaboratively how to create an inclusive classroom that supports the success of everyone.

Spontaneous Home Language Moments

Some L1 moments can be planned, like the bilingual teaching strategies on p. 36 or the Practice ideas throughout this book, but others may arise spontaneously as a natural part of responsive teaching. Responsive teaching keeps learning and meaning making at the center of instructional practice and flexibly responds to changes in student needs throughout the course of a day, so teachers should remain open to utilizing a student's full language repertoire should the need spontaneously arise. If you notice a student disengaging or struggling to complete a task in English, consider whether encouraging that student to utilize their full range of linguistic resources would help reengage them or make the task more manageable. Remember that L1 is a useful scaffold for both English language and literacy development and content learning. Creating links between existing knowledge and new knowledge makes input in English more comprehensible.

Whether L1 time is planned or naturally arises, it is important to understand the purpose of its use. Both teachers and students should reflect on what languages could be used for different purposes and what the implications of language choices might be. It is likely that our ELs have much to teach us about why they use different languages for different purposes. The idea that L1 is only ever used to compensate for a breakdown in English knowledge comes from the deficit perspective we need to resist. Provide students some room to decide which language(s) to use and ask them to justify their choices. Explore and examine language practices collaboratively with your students and use what you learn to inform your teaching.

Four Factors To Consider When Making Instructional Decisions Related to Home Language Use

Here are four questions adapted from Cook (2001) related to four factors (efficiency, learning, real-world relevance, and social justice) to consider when making instructional decisions around the use of students' L1. These four factors will help you to make decisions about whether L1 should be an explicit part of a particular classroom moment.

1. **Can this be done more effectively through the L1? (Efficiency)**
   Excluding L1 to maximize a student's exposure to English is hardly worth it if the student spends extended periods of time trying to understand the content in English and still fails to grasp the learning point. One example of this is deducing word meaning from context (see p. 10 for more on using L1 for vocabulary acquisition). In certain circumstances, L1 use frees up valuable class time that can be spent on more pedagogically beneficial learning tasks in English. It also mitigates unnecessary frustration or anxiety. Think about the purpose of the lesson. Consider if having a student practice English in that moment is more important than having them achieve the learning objective and acquire the content knowledge alongside their classmates or vice versa.

2. **Will L1 use in this circumstance support the development of language and literacy skills and/or curricular content knowledge? (Learning)**

The use of L1 facilitates transfer of knowledge and literacy skills to English. Consider whether drawing on L1 and all the knowledge encoded within would help a student to understand the content, vocabulary, or language structure being taught. If you are unsure, encourage the student to use their L1 to make connections to the learning happening in class and see if it helps. Part of navigating an openly multilingual classroom is experimenting with what works and what doesn't. How we go about maximizing the learning potential of each student looks different depending on the unique resources that the student brings into the classroom and how they respond to the task and various learning strategies.

3. **Will L1 use in this circumstance help students achieve the specific language competencies that they will need in the outside world? (Real-World Relevance)**

Students who can communicate and are literate in more than one language are better prepared to participate in a multilingual society and increasingly internationally integrated global economy. Producing competent bi-/multilinguals should be a stated goal and source of pride in education. Reconceptualizing the end goal for ELs (achieving native-like English vs. achieving proficiency in more than one language) changes how we respond to the use of languages other than English in the classroom. Consider whether an instructional decision you make in the moment disregards or recognizes the value of bilingualism and biliteracy. These are skills that will serve students not only academically, but also in their families, communities, and future workplaces.

4. **Will L1 use in this circumstance promote equity and inclusion? Will it contribute to leveling the playing field for ELs? (Social Justice)**

L1 plays a significant role in leveling the playing field for ELs by enabling them to engage with complex and creative work to the same full extent as their native-English-speaking peers. It is a tool of inclusion and empowerment. When ELs are restricted to English-only, they have fewer resources to draw on for learning purposes; a large portion of their voice is silenced. Where monolingual English children are permitted unrestricted access to all their linguistic resources for learning, ELs are constrained by what they are able to accomplish with partial access. Instruction should use L1 to provide more equitable opportunities for ELs and bilingual students to learn and excel academically. These instructional decisions are inextricably linked to social justice.

Turn-Taking: Make Space for All Voices to Be Heard (All levels)
Disrupt inequitable interaction patterns in your lessons that inadvertently favor native English speakers. One example of how to do this is to make sure that turn-taking patterns allow for all students' voices to be a part of classroom learning conversations. Listen for the quiet students in the classroom (in an English-only setting, often ELs), and find ways to amplify their voices. If students can use their

L1 to communicate, they can participate more fully and meaningfully in classroom discussions. If you do not speak the L1(s) of your students, elicit the help of a digital translation tool or same-L1 peer to help translate. The use of L1 in this circumstance advances social justice in the classroom.

Scenario: Putting Yourself in Your Students' Shoes

(From "Help or Hindrance? Use of Native Language in the English Classroom," by E. Hermann, n.d., *MultiBriefs Exclusive* [www.multibriefs.com/briefs/exclusive/help_or _hindrance.html]. Reprinted with permission.)

You and a few colleagues have decided to move to a foreign country, one in which you do not speak the language. As part of your preparation, you begin studying the language of the country, researching the culture and traditions, etc.

Once there, you and your colleagues take a local university course that explains the school system, cultural attitudes towards schooling, and other issues related to education in the country. The challenge for you and your colleagues is that the course is taught in a language you do not yet speak or understand well.

Throughout the course, the teacher does his best job to make the input comprehensible, interesting, and relevant. You are engaged throughout the instruction and understand, at least at a basic level, the instruction provided. Throughout each lesson, there are ample opportunities for you to turn and talk to colleagues about the content being presented.

During these interactions with your peers, what language are you most likely to use: English or the language of the country/instruction? For most people, if they were asked to speak to their colleagues or friends who speak the same language, they would speak in the language they were most comfortable with and that they know best. In this case, that would be English. When the teacher asks you to share your discussions, you might then attempt to explain, in the language of instruction, what you discussed with your partner....

The ability to speak to others in English to clarify key ideas such as similarities and differences in the school systems, how the information relates to you and your experience, how the content affects your planning, and other ideas would be a benefit as it would help in deepening your comprehension of the topic. If you are an educator, high levels of background knowledge of the content area (in this case educational systems) would have aided your comprehension. Although there might be new information presented, it would most likely fit into your existing schema and therefore be easier to comprehend and recall....

Because you would still be learning the language of instruction, including academic terms, phrases, and other vocabulary along with potentially complex language forms and structures, learning in this environment would be more challenging. Imagine if the teacher did not give you the opportunity to clarify the key concepts, questions, and topics before they called on you to share.

In this situation, you would have to process the content and language very quickly and attempt to formulate your response in a new language when being called upon by the teacher. As you process information being shared, you would also need to put effort into how you were going to share the information: the vocabulary, phrases, and sentences you would attempt to use to communicate. Depending on the make-up of the class, your comfort level, and the support the teacher provides, the classroom may feel like a safe place to take risks in communicating in a new language or it may feel uncomfortable to take risks.

 After reading the preceding scenario, ask yourself: What may have helped you in this scenario? What may have been difficult in this scenario? Pausing to empathize with the everyday challenges your ELs encounter in the classroom on a regular basis will help you to make strategic and caring instructional decisions around the use of their L1.

Bilingual Teaching Strategies

 Grade 11 social studies teacher and monolingual native English speaker, Stephanie, describes her multilingual approach in the classroom: "When I first started teaching, I was really nervous that I couldn't understand everything my students said. I kept thinking, 'How can I teach them if I can't understand them?' Now though, I just let them go if they're on a roll—if I can tell they're really into a discussion or a debate, I just sit back and listen. Later, if I feel like it's something I can build on, I'll ask a student like Teresita or Eddy to fill me in on what I missed." (García et al., 2017, p. 126)

You do not need to be bilingual to implement bilingual teaching strategies. Will inviting students' L1s into the classroom involve giving up a degree of control? Yes, but letting go of the traditional authoritative role and giving students greater independence and agency over their own learning can build their self-confidence, produce improved academic outcomes, and promote positive teacher-student relationships. A common question of teachers who do not speak the L1s of their students is: "How will I know what my students are talking about if I don't speak the language they are using?" This is a valid concern, but one that can be mitigated by utilizing a few simple strategies. The following tips have been adapted from Hermann (n.d.).

1. **Be specific.** When providing instructions for a group or pair task, be very explicit and clear in the prompt; for example, "Discuss three important points about . . . ," "Find two examples of . . . ." When a specific prompt is given, students are more likely to stay on task.

2. **Listen.** Listen to students as they are speaking. You will hear a general lull in the noise level at some point. This is an indication that the group has finished discussing the topic given and are starting to discuss other things. Additionally, listen to the English-speaking students in the class. When they begin wrapping up their discussions, it is likely that other students are doing the same.

3. **Observe body language.** In any language, if students are off topic or discussing something inappropriate to the task, you will often see them glancing at the teacher to check if they know that other things are being discussed. Subtle clues in body language or facial expressions can signal that the group is not on task.

4. **Assign a task.** To compel additional accountability, assign a hands-on task for the group to complete during or after discussion, for example, answering comprehension questions, compiling a list, or creating a graphic organizer.

The following bilingual teaching strategies have been organized under the four major language skill areas (reading, writing, listening, and speaking). It is not just English as a second language (ESL) teachers that utilize these four language skills in their lessons—teachers of any subject in any context use them in their instruction and expect students to demonstrate their knowledge through these modalities in return. The following strategies are applicable across grade levels and content areas and none of them require the teacher to know the L1s of their students.

Home Language Across the Four Skill Areas (All levels)

Reading

- Pair students from the same language background to discuss difficult passages and grapple with complex texts using their L1.

- Provide L1 or dual-language books and encourage students to read them.

- Read dual-language texts as a whole class using ELs' language expertise to help translate.

- Encourage students to use bilingual resources to understand difficult material (e.g., bilingual dictionaries, dual-language literacy materials, digital apps including pronunciation aids and machine translators).

- Cocreate interactive multilingual word walls with your students (see p. 14 for more on these).

Writing

- Encourage ELs to prewrite using their L1 or both languages (e.g., a bilingual graphic organizer or essay outline). This can be done independently or in same-L1 peer groups.

 Evidence suggests that students who use their L1 to brainstorm ideas and construct first drafts subsequently write pieces in English that are considerably more developed than their usual ESL writing. (Wang & Wen, 2002)

- Students practice writing for a bilingual audience by creating dual-language texts. Group students from the same language background so that those with more advanced English proficiency can help those with early emergent English. Dual-language texts create greater potential for students to produce more complex, creative, and personally relevant work which often results in increased motivation and engagement in learning. Greater student engagement leads to greater student achievement.

- Have students read or tell stories in their L1 and then translate them into English to read to other students.

- Engage students in activities that compare features of different languages. Encourage students to be "language ethnographers" and provide spaces to reflect on their own language practices and purposes. This promotes metalinguistic awareness for everyone in the classroom, monolingual students included.

- Give students opportunities to practice applying new knowledge and skills in low-pressure contexts. L1 use can help with this, as can assigning ungraded, peer-evaluated, or pass/fail assignments to encourage students to experiment with new styles of thinking, writing, and learning.

Speaking

- Give same-L1 students time to discuss a topic or task using their L1 (e.g., think, pair, share in L1). A few minutes of stress-free L1 discussion in pairs or small groups can lead to substantially extended English speaking. Cooperative work using L1 allows students to negotiate meaning and deliberate on language choices before switching to English.

- Provide opportunities for students to showcase their emerging bilingual skills by using their complete language repertoire when speaking (e.g., students write and perform dual-language poems or plays or deliver bilingual class presentations).

- Encourage students to discuss schoolwork at home and get help from family members using their L1.

- Hold student-teacher conferences, particularly with early emergent ELs, in the L1 or a combination of L1 and English. Without reciprocal dialogue and mutual understanding, there is little value in feedback and limited opportunity for students to demonstrate their ability to use it constructively. Use an online translation tool or bilingual colleague or volunteer to facilitate. If this is not possible, have same-L1 classmates or upper grade mentors work together to give peer feedback and/or provide clarification on teacher feedback.

- As much as possible, grant ELs the right to be silent. Frequently, as educators, we (or curricular objectives) demand that students immediately begin to produce English as proof that they are making progress. It is important to recognize that just because a student is quiet, it does not mean they are not learning. More likely, they are building up competence by listening and gaining comprehension. Often, when an EL begins to speak English, it is not the beginning of their learning, but testimony to the learning they have already done. Allow students the time to process, internalize, and feel comfortable verbalizing to help create the kind of safe environment that is a critical part of language learning and learning in general.

Listening

- Provide space and time for students to discuss what they heard together using their L1.

- Encourage older, print-literate students to take class notes in their L1 or a combination of their L1 and English.

- In secondary or adult learning environments, record class sessions using Panopto (www.panopto.com) or another lecture capture tool so that students can replay the lecture at home or in class with or without subtitles. Many digital lecture capture tools provide computer-generated closed captioning with a high (80–90%) accuracy rate.

- Use students' L1 to communicate task instructions. Elicit the help of a bilingual teacher or student or use a machine translation tool to facilitate (e.g., the Google translate app on an iPad) and to ensure ELs clearly comprehend what is being asked of them. Using students' L1 for this purpose means that ELs do not begin an activity at an immediate disadvantage because they have no (or only partial) understanding of the instructions. They are not excluded from fully participating because of their language practices. Knowing precisely what the objectives of a task are and how they are expected to get there places ELs on more equal footing with their non-EL peers.

Older Students

 "From the teacher's point of view, planning and providing instruction on the basis of children's existing competencies and using experiences and knowledge that are familiar to the learner provide a solid foundation for extending children's skills and knowledge in new directions. From the second language student's point of view, learning on the basis of established skills and known experiences provides a reassuring context in which to acquire new skills and concepts." (Genesee, 1994, p. 3)

People use what they know to construct new understanding. The need for a reassuring context in which to acquire new skills and concepts does not dissipate with age—if anything, it intensifies. Adolescents and adults are often more self-conscious than very young children who readily make mistakes without fear of embarrassment. Children, for the most part, are unaware of language; it is secondary to whatever they are using it for. Their mistakes aren't continually corrected and, most important, they're allowed to be silent (Palfreman, 1983). An adolescent student or adult learner in mainstream or ESL programs, on the other hand, must progress at a rapid pace. These students are judged on their productive language skills from the moment they enter the classroom, and very often language itself is the focus, rather than the task it is being used for.

Beyond the program-based challenges of compressing a lot of learning into a short period of time, older students often have a greater fear of making mistakes, taking risks, and being vulnerable to judgement. Older learners also compare themselves more to native speakers. As Cummins et al. (2012) point out, there is active pressure on newcomer students to assimilate into main-stream society and to become just like their perception of "everybody else." It is not something to be ignored or taken lightly, as it often results in the erasure of students' beliefs, language, culture, traditions [*sic*] in essence, their identity. (p. 40)

This makes it even more crucial that students' L1s are validated and utilized as legitimate resources for academic learning. If teachers do not use students' language and background to bridge school-based language and literacy expectations, students will be at higher risk of alienation and underachievement. Using existing competencies as a foundation to extend new learning provides learners *of all ages* a secure jumping-off point, one that affirms students' identities, builds confidence, and gives them agency in their own learning; students don't enter the classroom as "deficient," but instead with much of value to contribute to their own learning and others'.

Students With Limited or Interrupted Formal Education

We know that L1 language and literacy skills transfer to additional language (L2) language and literacy skills, but what about for students with no or low literacy in their L1? Is the use of L1 still beneficial? Research has shown that the value of L1 inclusion in learning is potentially even greater for students with limited or interrupted formal education (SLIFE; Carlo & Sylvester, 1996; Condelli et al., 2009). When there is strategic focus on developing students' L1 literacy, they not only benefit from the identity affirmation that happens when they have their language and background validated at school, they also develop skills that will transfer to English language and literacy development.

SLIFE will have typically participated in much different learning environments and will have developed ways of thinking and learning that are much different from those expected and valued in formal education. For example, for many of these students, learning is often situated in the family and community and is based on a cyclical mentoring or apprenticeship model: demonstration, practice, feedback, and more practice until mastery has been achieved (Mejía-Arauz et al., 2012). Their learning is not typically grounded in print-based literacy. Instead, information may have most often been communicated orally and nonverbally in the same moment that the learner is observing or participating in the process (Paradise & Rogoff, 2009); learning is connected to experiences in real time. Learners and mentors also frequently have a close relationship; they are usually members of the same community and know each other personally. In contrast, teachers in the U.S. school system are often removed from their students' lives outside of school. Close relationships between teachers and students, particularly in secondary school, constitute the exception rather than the rule. Learning is characterized by formal problem-solving (scientific reasoning) that involves abstract thinking (e.g., categorization, classification), often detached from personal experiences and the concrete world. Formal, Western-style education is also predicated on literacy, literacy that is narrowly defined as print based (e.g., reading pages of text) and monolingual (English). This difference between ways of learning, understanding, and interacting with others often leads to confusion and isolation among SLIFE, which are often interpreted as a lack of effort or ability by teachers.

The deficit narratives that frequently accompany these students, characterized by what they lack (e.g., English proficiency, print literacy, subject-area knowledge), are because their assets are almost always invisible when viewed through the lens of formal education (DeCapua, 2016). We must remember that SLIFE lack academic experiences, but not life experiences. Many SLIFE have a pragmatic rather than academic approach to learning (DeCapua & Marshall, 2009). The significant knowledge and skills these students have acquired through prior lived experiences may not be the same as those expected by teachers in North American schools, but they are the cornerstone of a successful transition to formal education and integral to enhancing the education of the other students in the classroom and school community as a whole.

As teachers of culturally and linguistically diverse students, we must keep at front of mind that different cultures often choose from different modalities for learning and meaning making. Both multilingual and multimodal approaches are central to ensuring SLIFE are included at school and their rich funds of knowledge are valued and built upon. "Funds of knowledge" (González et al., 2005) refers to the skills and knowledge that have been culturally developed and accumulated over time to enable an individual or household to function within a given culture. Integrating these funds of knowledge into classroom activities is essential for creating a richer and more highly scaffolded learning environment. If a teacher is aware that a student may not understand something as it is presented on a one-dimensional page in a book but may have extensive experience with that concept in real life, they can attempt to embed the learning in a familiar context using oral instructions and permit the student to explicitly draw on their L1 to scaffold learning, for example, linking mathematics to making change, pricing services, or portioning and ratios.

 Think about a concept in the curriculum that is abstract. Consider that for many SLIFE, learning is experiential—for many of these students, learning happens in a real-world context, so decontextualized content may present a challenge. How could you create some context (i.e., immediate relevance) to provide support for students to achieve the same learning objective for your lesson using a different path to get there (i.e., framing the problem differently or using a different process)?

ELs, especially SLIFE, might possess skills and knowledge that lie outside of what is traditionally valued at school. It is crucial for teachers to recognize those resources, be open to learning about them, and be willing to experiment with how to best utilize them in support of school-based learning.

Home Language and Learning in the Digital Age

Two of the principal forces shaping teaching and learning in North America today are increasingly diverse, multilingual student bodies and the widespread use of digital technologies as tools for communication and meaning making. Traditionally, human, face-to-face interaction accompanied by text-based material has been the standard channel for (language) learning. The digital age has changed this, though, both through the channel and the modality of transmission. The ways in which a generation of digital natives learns language and content material best is different than it used to be. It is important, then, to find ways in the classroom to draw on students' interests and prior knowledge to actively engage them in learning. The discussion and practice ideas presented next demonstrate just a few of the ways that L1 can be productively integrated into students' digital realities.

Harnessing Machine Translation as a Learning Tool

Machine translation (MT) is everywhere. The world's most popular MT application, Google Translate, has more than 500 million users and translates an average of 100 billion words per day across 100 languages. Google's Pixel Buds can translate between 40 different languages literally in real time, search engines offer to translate entire webpages for you with the click of a mouse, and mobile texting platforms can translate as you type. MT accuracy will only continue to get better, challenging teachers in increasingly multilingual classrooms to confront and adapt to the realities of how students are engaging with translation tools in the digital age. Though still controversial, it is likely that the capabilities of translation technology will impel educators to find ways to reframe MT as a tool to enhance human capabilities rather than replace them. "The highest and best use of technology is not to eliminate the need for language learning, but to facilitate it" (America the Bilingual, 2020, para. 7). If used appropriately, the process a student engages in with a machine translator (e.g., negotiating between languages, noticing differences and equivalences) becomes just as important, if not more important, than the final product.

 Stephanie Jones, Grade 3 teacher at Chris Hadfield Public School, talks about the impact of a pilot project she was involved with using Google Translate in the classroom: "Before, if you asked a student if they understood, they would nod their head in agreement and then you'd go and check their work and you'd see they didn't understand. Now I can ask what do you understand and what don't you understand. I can then work with what the student knows . . . The Google tool makes students feel included . . . [My EL student] is doing exactly what everyone else is doing and it makes a more inclusive environment for her when she's able to use her own language . . . The kids love using the technology and using it with her. They use it for classwork, but also to talk to each other at lunch. They pass the phone around and they're giggling away. It's wonderful to see." (Riedner, 2018)

Three Versions **(Grades 4–12, adult)**
Ask ELs to create three versions of a response to a text that is being worked on in class—an L1 version, an English version in the student's own words, and a Google Translate version. Create a shared, collaborative online document (e.g., using Google Docs) with four columns. The first column should include the reading strategy the student is working on, for example, comprehension questions based on the text. The student writes L1 responses in the second column, English responses in the third column (using the English they know), and Google Translate versions in the fourth column. A shared document like this facilitates collaboration between student and teacher. It also allows the teacher to view the revision history to gain insight into how the student negotiated between languages to complete the task, using the translator to edit vocabulary or make corrections to their English version or vice versa. You will

find that students can often analyze the accuracy of the machine translated output and decide what changes to make to their own English responses.

This activity places value on responses in the L1 as well as those written in English. It also utilizes MT, a technology that many ELs already use, whether it is explicitly condoned by classroom policy or not, in a positive way—one that helps students refine their own language and develop biliteracy skills. See an example by Chinese student Fu-han, who used Google Translate during writing activities in a mainstream Grade 6 language arts classroom in the United States (Figure 1).

Responses to "THE EMPTY POT"

Reading strategy (阅读策略)	中文	在回应自己的话 (Respond in English in your own words.)	English (Google Translate)
Did someone realize something? How might this change things?	男孩注意到了他的种子长不出来，这样他可能会失去变成皇帝的继承人的机会。	The boy found the seed is not growing, he think he may not be the emperor's heir.	The boy found his species does not grow, he felt could not be the emperor's heir.
What have you learned about a character? How do you know this?	男孩是一个很诚实的孩子，因为他的种子是长不出来的，所以他就拿着一个空的花蓝去见皇上。	the boy is a honest kid, because the seed is can't growing, so he just take a empty pots go to see the emperor	The boy is a very honest boy, because his seed is not out long, so he took an empty pot to see the emperor.
What themes do you notice? Why?	这个故事围绕着小孩和种子，因为这个故事大部分在讲小孩想了什么办法让种子长大。	The story is about the boy and his seed, because the story talking about what the boy wanted to let the seeds grow method.	The story revolves around children and seeds, because the kids want to tell the story mostly in what way to let the seeds grow.

Figure 1. Google Translate writing activity example. From "An expanded view of translanguaging: Leveraging the dynamic interactions between a young multilingual writer and machine translation software," by S. Vogel, L. Ascenzi-Moreno, & O. García, in J. Choi & S. Ollerhead (Eds.), *Plurilingualism in teaching and learning* (pp. 105–122). Copyright 2018, Routledge. Reproduced by permission of Taylor & Francis Group through PLSclear.

The research team (Vogel et al., 2018) worked with Fu-han's teacher, Ross, and encouraged him to recognize Fu-han's engagement with Google Translate as a "'legitimate biliteracy instance' (Hornberger, 2003) that needed support" (p. 98). With the help of the researchers, Ross created a shared online document that required Fu-han to provide several different versions of responses to comprehension questions about "The Empty Pot," a story he was reading in class. Ross was able to track Fu-han's progress as he worked through the questions, which gave him insight into the processes Fu-han engaged in to negotiate between the languages in his repertoire to successfully complete the activity.

Affirming Biliterate Identities With English Learners Through Digital Storytelling

Digital storytelling is a powerful way to build school-based literacy for emerging readers and writers. Digital stories offer opportunities for students to construct multimodal narratives that reflect their interests and lives outside of the classroom. These creative projects provide an engaging format for students to develop their identities as authors/designers and increase participation in literacy at school. The multimodality of digital stories expands the possibilities for students' expression and exposition, which is particularly important when we remember that different cultures often select different modalities for learning and meaning making. Literacy learning does not occur in a vacuum—children and adolescents bring their own cultural resources, histories, and purposes to the process; their literacy practices are deeply embedded within their own multiple and dynamic identities and depend largely on context.

Digital storytelling relies on showing as much as it does on writing. Students can combine multiple media, including images (e.g., photos, graphics), text, oral narration, music, special effects, or video. Preliterate children can draw pictures and narrate their stories. Engaging for students of any age, digital stories are particularly beneficial for ELs and SLIFE, who can draw from their funds of knowledge, incorporate their L1, and choose from multiple modes to communicate.

The process of crafting digital stories provides teachers with valuable opportunities to connect students' prior knowledge to academic learning in any language. There are several easy-to-use digital tools that make digital storytelling possible for all students, including those in elementary grades and those with limited digital literacy, for example:

- Glogster (www.edu.glogster.com)

- PechaKucha (www.pechakucha.com)

- Wixie (www.wixie.com)

- StoryboardThat (www.storyboardthat.com)

Many digital storytelling tools include a storyboard view that displays the pages in a project, which helps students to see how their visuals and writing are organized and to change the order of events and ideas. These storytelling apps can be used to tell the stories themselves (e.g., StoryboardThat is particularly good for creating digital comic strips) or they can be used to facilitate the planning of projects using the storyboard template.

Ask students to collect artifacts (e.g., photographs, videos, images, quotations) for their stories, create a storyboard on paper or using one of the aforementioned applications, and then use a free video creation/editing software like iMovie (for Mac; www.apple.com/imovie) or FilmoraGo (for Mac and Windows; filmora.wondershare .com/filmorago-video-editing-app) to create a video. These applications have user-friendly interfaces that allow students to add text, narration, music, transitions, and effects to their stories. Students can create and edit their videos from a computer, laptop, tablet, or mobile device.

Digital Storytelling Project Ideas

Digital stories can take a variety of forms, from creative or information pieces to opinion-based, instructional, or autobiographical pieces. They will often meet cross-curricular standards and can be tailored to specific subject areas. You may opt to have students explore a particular theme or create a story in response to a specific question.

Autobiography (All levels)

Students craft a narrative about their life to date. Give students plenty of freedom to invest their identities in these projects, choose what they want to include/exclude, and how they want to carry them out. ELs can create dual-language stories that reflect their bi-/multilingual realities and history.

Very Important Person (All levels)

Students describe an influential person in their life (e.g., a member of their immediate or extended family or community) and why that person is significant to them. ELs should be encouraged to use their L1 and English (e.g., they can interview their very important person, or VIP, in their L1 and translate pieces of dialogue into English in their story). A project like this not only gives students the opportunity to bring their family and community into the classroom but also provides teachers with valuable insight into their students' lives outside of the classroom.

How-To (All levels)

Students create a how-to tutorial using digital storytelling to give step-by-step instructions. Students are positioned as the experts on a topic of their choosing, which validates their funds of knowledge and connects them to school-based literacy. Teachers can connect students' real-life know-how to academic skills like organizing and sequencing. These projects include a series of pages that contains simple text and/or oral narration (encourage ELs to use both their L1 and English) along with supporting visuals (i.e., photos or illustrations). PowToon (www.powtoon.com) is a good digital platform to use for this project. Students might choose to share how they cook a favorite meal, play an instrument, do henna, take the perfect jump shot, and so on.

Creative Writing (All levels)

Students create an original story or retell a folk story with the option of creating dual-language stories. They could translate a popular English story into their L1 or vice versa, write in both their L1 and L2, or include voice recordings from family or community members in their L1. Depending on proficiency level, ELs can work independently (with teacher support), in same-L1 peer groups, or cocreate their story with parents or caregivers.

Because sounds and images are as important to digital stories as text, creative writing using this platform is often less intimidating to ELs (including SLIFE). They can draw on oral traditions and visual representations to tell their stories. In fact, they can narrate their stories without having to write at all. Alternatively, they can voice record their ideas, find a parent or peer to help with adding text, and then work to edit the printed version before recording again.

Give students' products value outside of the classroom by publishing them as hard copies or eBooks and posting them on an online platform (e.g., school website, class website, or blog), displaying them on the shelf in the school library, or having students read them to younger children in the school. By reaching broader audiences, students' products are given real-life utility. They get a sense that the work they do in the classroom actually matters and has practical value in the wider world. In the process, their identities as competent biliterate and bilingual individuals are affirmed.

Examples of digital storytelling projects:

- I am plurilingual! Je suis plurilingue! (www.iamplurilingual.com/e-books.html)

- Critical Connections: Multilingual Digital Storytelling Project (goldsmithsmdst.com/showcase)

- StoryCenter: United States (www.storycenter.org/stories)

- StoryCentre: Canada (www.storycentre.ca/stories)

Chapter 2 Review

In an interview with adolescent ELs, Vogt (2020) asked: "If you could tell teachers one thing that they could do to make it easier for you as an English learner, what would it be?" A young woman from India said, "Don't just talk to the kids who speak English. Talk to us, too." A boy from Ukraine said, "Tell us what to do in the order we have to do it." Finally, a girl from Guatemala paused and then quietly added, "I would tell them to not forget we're here." (p. 340)

For teachers in English-medium, mainstream K–12 classrooms, teaching to a linguistically diverse group of students without adequate preparation can pose professional challenges. Even instructors specializing in teaching ELs can struggle with issues such as how to effectively respond to variations in competency across the four skill areas at the individual level and variations in proficiency across a given student group. Teachers in any context may have moments when they are simply at a loss for ways to make content accessible and help students in their classroom develop the English language and literacy skills they need to succeed.

Chapter 1 provided a knowledge base for understanding why the inclusion of L1 is so essential to student success. Chapter 2 dealt with the practical issues of integrating languages other than English into classroom learning—the how and when of L1 in day-to-day instruction. The information and suggestions presented in this chapter provided a flexible framework that can be customized to your individual student group and instructional approaches. Modifying lesson plans, teaching techniques, and classroom activities to recognize and integrate students' entire language repertoire and out-of-school competencies may seem daunting at first, particularly for those teachers with well-established routines and ways of teaching that have proven successful. However, it is salient to recognize that good teaching is not always good enough for everyone. And, though educational change will require the work of multiple levels of the educational system, as well as government and policymakers, teachers have an important role to play in generating greater educational equity for these students.

CHAPTER 3

HOME LANGUAGE AND TESOL'S
THE 6 PRINCIPLES FOR EXEMPLARY
TEACHING OF ENGLISH LEARNERS®

TESOL's 6 Principles (TESOL International Association, 2018) define a set of core tenets to follow for effective English language education; they detail how educators of any age level and subject can create optimal conditions for productive social and academic language development for English learners (ELs). The 6 Principles are highly compatible with adopting an openly multilingual approach in the classroom, regardless of the teacher's own language background. This chapter discusses the benefits of home language (L1) and how it can be practically integrated into each of The 6 Principles:

1. Know your learners

2. Create conditions for language learning

3. Design high-quality lessons for language development

4. Adapt lesson delivery as needed

5. Monitor and assess student language development

6. Engage and collaborate within a community of practice

Classroom practices involving L1 that are useful in implementing and supporting each principle are identified with examples provided throughout this chapter.

Principle 1: Know Your Learners

Teachers cannot make use of students' funds of knowledge if they do not know what they are. It is only once we learn about our students' prior knowledge, skills, and varied life experiences that we can make those crucial connections between what they already bring to the classroom and what is required of them to succeed in formal schooling.

"Recognizing a person's prior knowledge is another manner of recognizing the person." (Brooks-Lewis, 2009, p. 228)

Often, much of ELs' knowledge is encoded in their L1, so integrating L1 or dual-language activities that encourage students to draw on that knowledge not only validates who they are and what they bring to the classroom but also leverages their existing resources to support and enhance classroom learning. Moreover, L1 may be a necessary part of getting to know ELs with early emergent English. Restricting students to English only can greatly limit what they are able to express about themselves and what they need to learn effectively in the classroom. It also limits the extent to which teachers can involve families and make connections to students' homes and communities in the course of their learning.

Using Home Language to Involve Families

Family involvement is an integral part of a child's success at school. Including L1 can transform the kind of involvement family members have in their child's schooling and, conversely, transform the kind of experience children have at school. Using L1s enables families to actively support their children's literacy development through conversation, reading, storytelling, and play, regardless of caregivers' English proficiency. Students can bring home L1 or dual-language books to read, including their own bilingual writing, and teachers can invite families to watch bilingual performances in class. Caregivers with low or no English can help their child complete schoolwork, and teachers can bring familial input and experiences to the classroom. Using students' L1 creates opportunities for students to showcase their language skills in the classroom and at home, fostering pride in students' emerging bilingualism. Family members become collaborators with both their children and their children's teachers. To develop positive relationships with families throughout the school year, teachers can do the following:

- **Meet with families.** Meet with families at the beginning of the year either at school or at a home visit, if possible. A face-to-face meeting is much more effective than sending home a questionnaire or having a brief informal conversation. Initiate and maintain dialogue and relationships with families that focus on the importance of both L1 and English language and literacy development.

- **Utilize technology.** Use a parent-teacher app like ClassDojo (www.classdojo.com) or Remind (www.remind.com) to communicate with parents and share classroom moments. Messages sent in English can be automatically translated. Students can help less tech-savvy parents navigate these apps or, alternatively, teachers can print out screenshots with translations included to share with parents periodically (e.g., at parent-teacher conferences).

- **Communicate in the home language.** Send home welcome letters, monthly calendars, classroom forms, and other information in students' L1s whenever possible. If you don't speak the language(s) of your students, use a translation tool to help, and ask colleagues or parents to proofread. It is a lot of extra work initially, but you will quickly build a stock of resources in multiple languages that you can reuse with minor revisions.

- **Use journals.** Send home two-way journals for families to read, write in, and return using both their L1 and English. It is okay if you do not understand what has been written. Use an online translator to help or ask your student to help translate.

- **Invite speakers.** Invite family members of students to speak to the class (e.g., on a Career Day where parent volunteers visit the class and talk with students about their jobs). If possible, facilitate presentations in languages other than English by arranging for an interpreter to attend. Personally reach out to caregivers of ELs for added encouragement and to assure them that their presence is valued regardless of the language they present in.

- **Welcome family members.** Invite parents or caregivers to classroom events, such as end-of-unit celebrations, project presentations, reader's theater performances, or awards ceremonies. Make these classroom events bilingual whenever possible (i.e., encourage ELs to use both languages in performances and projects).

For other ideas on how to involve families, see the following three Practice ideas.

Because caregivers of ELs may hold many of the same assumptions about learning as educators do (see Chapter 1 for common assumptions about language learning), they may want their children to be immersed in an English-only environment at school. It is important to stress to them the importance of maintaining and developing L1 language and literacy skills. Explain how skills and knowledge transfer from one language to another and share the well-documented academic advantages of L1 literacy in learning a new language (August & Shanahan, 2006). To guide families in becoming active supporters of their child's educational development, help parents and caregivers understand that reading in any language develops literacy across languages. We can help families recognize the many ways literacy is fostered every day at home using L1 and affirm the valuable role they play in their child's education. Story sacks and other activities, like the collaborative creation of dual-language texts, build on and extend family literacy practices and, importantly, signal to families that talking, reading, and writing in any language strengthens literacy development and contributes to overall intellectual growth.

"Children's linguistic and cultural identities should be affirmed by creating inclusive environments, where words in all languages become foundations for learning." (Catibusic-Finnegan, 2017, para. 10)

Story Sacks (Grades K–6)

A story sack is typically a large cloth bag containing a book along with supporting materials that stimulate reading activities and help make sharing the book more engaging and interactive. Creating story sacks with children and caregivers is an excellent way to support families as collaborators in learning, regardless of their English proficiency. Include dual-language or L1 books for ELs. Props might include soft toys or puppets of the main characters, an audio or video recording of the story, a related nonfiction book, or costumes and props for acting out the story. An idea card with prompts and story extender activities for family members and children to do together is also included. The idea card might include comprehension questions about the story, crafts that relate to the story, a language or matching game connected to the story, board games, or rhymes or songs on a shared theme. Include a checklist of everything in the story sack to ensure all items are returned.

If possible, translate idea cards into different languages with help from families, school staff, or a machine translator. You can also include images of each step or record a video on YouTube, for example, and provide the link in the story sack to help mitigate language or literacy barriers.

Story sacks can take the pressure off caregivers who do not have strong literacy skills. When using a story sack, it is not necessary to read the story word for word. Children and parents can use the props and characters in the story to act it out or make up their own stories and endings. Moreover, a book is not a mandatory part of this activity. Story sacks are also an excellent way to tell traditional oral stories and make them come to life for children. This can be especially useful for cultures whose literacy practices are based in oral tradition. Creating story sacks for oral stories can be done just as you would do for a picture book, except the audio recording becomes more important as the resource used to learn and practice the story. Alternatively, you could create a story sack of just props and encourage families to create their own stories (in any language) based on the items they find in the bag. To see how this might be done, watch "Story bag—How to tell stories with your kids" (www.youtube.com/watch?v= -QlOGDeADuc).

Invite families to add their own props and resources to the bag. Families can select familiar and culturally relevant materials to add to their story sack. Children can bring the story sack back to school and talk about the new items. The multimodal and multilingual nature of story sacks reinforces the significance of literacy activities in which children and families are already engaged—including those that are culturally diverse and in languages other than English. For story sack ideas, visit "National Literacy Trust—Story Sacks" (literacytrust.org.uk/resources/how-make-and-use-story-sack).

School-Home Correspondence

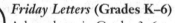

Friday Letters (Grades K–6)
Ask students in Grades 3–6 to write a letter that summarizes what they learned, found interesting, or liked best at school that week. Invite ELs to use their L1 or write bilingually. Teachers can scribe for students in K–2 classrooms and/or students can draw pictures of the week's highlights. Keep students' letters and/or pictures in a journal or folder and leave room for parents to respond. Encourage parents with low English proficiency to write in their L1 or a combination of L1 and English. A tool like Google Translate's instant camera translation can be used to translate parents' messages into English.

Classroom Newsletters (Grades 3–8)
Ask students to collect interesting artifacts, classroom materials, and bits of information in a file that will be used to prepare a newsletter that highlights the month's events. Have ELs create a bilingual newsletter or one in their L1.

Friday letters and bilingual monthly newsletters involve families regardless of their English proficiency through use of the L1 and reinforce the idea that writing in any language is valuable.

Using Home Language to Leverage the Resources That Students Bring to the Classroom to Enhance Learning

Our schools are rich with cultural, linguistic, and familial diversity. Infusing this diversity into a Eurocentric, English-language curriculum requires that teachers actively work to identify and include diverse cultures and languages in everyday classroom practice. Without this consistent and conscious effort, we risk alienating students and families and limiting opportunities for collaboration and community engagement. A student's underachievement is sometimes attributed to a mismatch between home and school. When a family's literacy practices, ways of knowing, and expectations are viewed as being incompatible with what is valued at school, families and students are marginalized. In contrast, when these differences are positioned as resources and invited into the classroom, children can make crucial connections between what happens at school and their interests, life experiences, and other aspects of their personalities and beliefs that make them who they are. Students' unique gifts and talents are legitimized and validated as assets at school and, in the process, their identities are affirmed.

English Learners as Language Brokers

Language brokering is a translanguaging practice (when speakers draw from their full language repertoire for a single conversation) in which children ". . . facilitate communication between two linguistically and/or culturally different parties. Unlike formal interpreters and translators, brokers mediate, rather than merely transmit, information" (Tse, 1996, p. 465). The contexts in which language brokering take place are varied (e.g., home, stores, banks, post offices, doctor's offices, government agencies) and can involve spoken and written forms. Although many children of immigrant families are acting as language brokers for friends and family members on a daily basis, it is a role that is generally overlooked at school. However, language brokering fosters the development of many of the same social and cognitive skills that are needed for academic success. These children are not merely repeating back word-for-word translations; they are reformulating messages to accurately transmit intended meaning. This communicative achievement requires numerous metalinguistic and cognitive skills, including a heightened sensitivity to audience, increased awareness of social convention, and enhanced attention to nonverbal behaviors. Language brokering youth must decipher body posture and facial expressions, contextual clues, and culturally appropriate meanings. They must also "synthesize, label, describe, ask for clarification, and gauge whether they have accurately understood and conveyed meanings correctly" (Pimental & Sevin, 2009, p. 17). The practice of interpreting contextual clues in a wide variety of settings has been shown to aid in the development of sophisticated language competencies.

Language Brokering and Academic Achievement

Language brokers often get extensive practice with literacy and numeracy throughout the course of everyday brokering practices. Those who read and interpret written documents utilize a number of reading strategies that are useful in a school context, including skimming and rereading for specific information, breaking words into component parts, making cognate connections, and knowing when to ask for help (Pimentel & Sevin, 2009). Mathematical skills like adding, subtracting, multiplying, dividing, measurement, and problem-solving are incorporated into routine experiences of making purchases, assisting with banking, negotiating prices for goods and services, and so on. These skills are academic in nature and may lead to advantages at school. Research shows that academic achievement is related to language brokering (Buriel et al., 1998; Chen et al., 2020). Active brokering has been significantly related to increased standardized test scores for reading and comprehension as well as mathematics (Dorner et al., 2007).

Language brokering is a good example of an out-of-school practice that can be integrated and nurtured in the school context. Although we must be mindful of when and how we might draw upon and showcase bilingual/EL students' talents as language brokers (i.e., students should never feel pressure to language broker or be put in a position to do so inappropriately, e.g., at a parent-teacher conference), it is a knowledge set that can and should be recognized and valorized as relevant to and reflective of academic proficiency.

In mixed-language classroom settings (e.g., bilingual/dual-language education), conditions are already in place for cross-cultural and cross-lingual language brokering to occur (i.e., ELs can broker for native English speakers and vice versa). In English-medium classrooms, such brokering requires purposeful integration by the teacher. Bilingual students and more advanced ELs can language broker for same-L1 emergent ELs within their own classroom (e.g., translating teacher instructions for a task), across classrooms in the same grade level (e.g., collaborations with sister classes), or across grade levels in mentorship projects (e.g., older bilingual students language broker for younger ELs). Teachers can also encourage students to share language brokering experiences and make connections between the skills they have developed through language brokering and in-class tasks. Translating the skills of bilingual children into improved academic outcomes means finding ways to build on home and community practices, like language brokering, in service of classroom learning.

Principle 2: Create Conditions for Language Learning

Creating a safe and inclusive classroom environment is a prerequisite for any kind of meaningful learning and especially for language learning—an inherent part of which involves taking risks (e.g., making mistakes, sounding "different," saying something outside of what is normally expected). Integrating L1s and home cultures is an essential part of building deep understandings as well as creating a safe and reassuring context for learning.

Using Home Language to Promote an Emotionally Positive Classroom Environment

Reducing anxiety and building trust are integral to creating the positive classroom conditions that promote effective (language) learning. Beyond scaffolding English language learning and enhancing performance in content areas, L1 use has been shown to reduce cognitive overload and learner anxiety, particularly when it is used to explain complex terminology, concepts, and grammatical structures (Bruen & Kelly, 2014). When ELs know that they can access their L1 to grapple with challenging material and/or clarify vocabulary or concepts, their anxiety decreases significantly. L1 use calms fears around not being able to fully comprehend task instructions, keep up with peers, or understand content material; it cultivates a less intimidating and more relaxed classroom atmosphere.

An emotionally positive learning environment also involves decisions related to the design of the physical classroom environment. Ensure multiple languages and cultures are represented on classroom walls, bulletin boards, and other spaces (see Multilingual Word Walls on p. 14 or Cocreate Multilingual Resources for Classroom Use on p. 12 for ideas).

"When classroom instruction opens up the space for learners to use the full repertoire of their cognitive and linguistic tools and feel confident about the legitimacy of using their L1 for academic purposes, then academic performance can increase dramatically." (Cummins et al., 2012, pp. 40–41)

Create an Inclusive Classroom Ethos (All levels)

Every student should have a sense of place at school and see themselves reflected in their learning environment. There are some simple things you can do in your classroom to cultivate a positive classroom ethos where diversity is recognized and valued, many of which involve students' L1.

- Ensure you know students' language background (e.g., by getting information from the Home Language Survey, engaging students in an initial conversation about the language[s] they speak at home and in their community, or having students write a language biography or create an identity self-portrait—see Identity Self-Portraits on p. 19 for a description).

- Ask students to create and post a short welcome message in their L1 at the beginning of the year to post in the classroom. For preliterate students, ask families to help by creating a message at home and sending it in with their child.

- Exhibit students' multilingual work on the walls of the classroom.

- Include classroom signs, posters, and labels in students' L1s.

- At the beginning of a new unit of study, encourage families to send in pictures or other artifacts that relate to the topic to display in the classroom. Carefully placed visual references help children see and interact with language and knowledge from their home culture on a daily basis.

- Post a world map that marks the different home countries and ancestral backgrounds represented in the classroom.

- Implement lessons and culminating projects that allow students to showcase their bilingual skills.

- Work with your school librarian to select books or resources in the L1s of your students that relate to curricular themes you are studying.

- Invite guest speakers from diverse cultural and linguistic backgrounds to speak to the class. If possible, facilitate presentations in languages other than English by arranging for an interpreter.

- If possible, provide students access to an online translation tool using either a mobile phone or a tablet. A translation app can facilitate classroom learning and teacher/peer interaction, which helps to mitigate potential isolation and alienation for newcomer/entering ELs.

- Pair new ELs with a peer mentor to help guide them through classroom routines and activities. If possible, pair same-L1 students together or provide mentors who do not speak their mentees' L1 with a machine translator.

- Create collaborative classroom contracts that involve students in classroom decision-making. These might include policies on the use of different languages and practicing of respect for different ways of doing and thinking. Post the contract in both English and students' L1s. This helps students to have a clear idea of what is expected of the teacher and themselves.

- Create opportunities to discuss, compare, and analyze different languages and language varieties. Have students teach the class how to say something in their L1 and compare it with equivalences in other languages, including English. Any exposure to language enhances cognitive capacity, so a multilingual classroom is beneficial for everyone.

See Appendix E: Promoting an Inclusive Multilingual Classroom Checklist.

Using Home Language to Enhance Motivation for Learning and Maintain High Expectations of Success for All Learners

Whether implicitly or explicitly conveyed, consciously or unconsciously held, the expectations we have for our students affect their achievement and motivation for learning, often profoundly. As discussed in Chapter 1, expectations affect our behaviors toward students which, in turn, impact students' opportunities to learn. Low-expectation students are generally provided with fewer chances to respond, more simplified instruction, greater criticism, and less support and caring (de Boer et al., 2018). Minoritized students and those from lower socioeconomic backgrounds appear to be more affected by negative expectations (Sorhagen, 2013).

Drawing on students' L1s and cultures in the classroom reflects an underlying belief that those resources are legitimate and valuable in an academic setting and communicates that powerful message to students. L1 equips students with a vital resource for learning; they can employ a greater variety of learning strategies, use L1 to break down complex content and tasks into manageable steps and processes, and build upon what they already know and can do. L1 also leads to fuller and more active participation, because students are not limited to doing only what they can achieve using English alone. Including L1 means that students are more appropriately and effectively supported in achieving. Teachers can communicate high expectations and students are better equipped to meet them.

Principle 3: Design High-Quality Lessons for Language Development

This principle speaks to the importance of designing lessons that

1. communicate clear outcomes;

2. incorporate varied approaches, techniques, and modalities;

3. involve authentic language use;

4. actively engage learners with relevant and meaningful content;

5. allow for differentiated instruction;

6. promote the use of learning strategies and critical thinking; and

7. promote students' self-regulated learning.

L1 has a vital role to play in assisting teachers in incorporating each of these elements into the design and delivery of lessons. In the following section, I describe how L1 can be used productively to support lesson planning for each of the aforementioned seven practices.

Using Home Language to Prepare Lessons With Clear Outcomes and Convey Them to Students

In a strictly English-only classroom environment, it is often difficult for teachers to differentiate between a student's inability to demonstrate learning and their inability to demonstrate learning in English. The significance of this quandary is discussed in greater depth under Principle 5: Monitor and Assess Student Language Development on pp. 67–70; however, it warrants a mention here. L1 creates opportunities for teachers to gain insight into a student's competencies and learning regardless of their proficiency in the language of instruction. If students can use L1 to demonstrate learning, teachers can prepare lessons that separate language proficiency from curriculum objectives, fairly assess student progress, better identify challenge areas, and clearly communicate objectives and feedback to students.

On an individual task level, English-only means that ELs might be asked to undertake an activity or assignment without a clear idea of what is expected. Being unable to clearly convey information is frustrating for both teachers and students, and it puts ELs at a disadvantage before they even begin. Having a classroom peer translate or using a machine translator to clearly communicate task instructions and expectations levels the playing field for ELs. It can make a significant difference to a student's engagement and in their ability to participate fully.

Using Home Language to Provide and Enhance Input Through Varied Approaches, Techniques, and Modalities

L1 provides multiple opportunities for students to receive comprehensible and enhanced input. Its inclusion in classroom learning opens up a multitude of new instructional strategies for teachers. When considering how to convey new information to students, in what ways (e.g., text, oral, video, inquiry) and with what support (e.g., using context, scaffolding), teachers can now involve L1 and culturally relevant materials that use L1 in making those consequential decisions.

As discussed throughout this book, L1 acts as a vital scaffold in helping students cope with unfamiliar content and new language. It can be used to clarify vocabulary and concepts, support students in accomplishing higher order thinking and classroom tasks, apply already developed learning strategies to contend with new material, and be used to create output (e.g., texts, oral presentations, multimedia) for multiple and varied audiences. Moreover, L1 is a tool to ensure students understand teacher input (e.g., by using translation tools or having a same-L1 peer or classroom volunteer use the L1) and to confirm and consolidate new learning. L1 can be leveraged in a variety of strategic ways to scaffold English language input.

As was emphasized in Chapter 1, languages do not occupy separate compartments in the minds of bilinguals but rather are integrated parts of a single, unified linguistic system. When we visualize languages in this way, we are better able to take advantage of the interaction that takes place between them to support learning. And remember, bilingual strategies are not only accessible to bilingual teachers; monolingual teachers can use students' L1 in productive ways, as well—the Practice ideas included throughout this book can be used by teachers of any language background.

Using Home Language to Engage Learners in the Use and Practice of Authentic Language

Although the value of connecting classroom learning to students' homes and communities is generally acknowledged among those in education, the connections that are considered valuable (e.g., home literacy, family involvement) rarely extend to the authentic language practices students engage in outside of the classroom. Teaching to the whole child is not limited to involving caregivers and family literacies using English; it also means including the language practices ELs engage in using languages other than English at home, with peer groups, and in their communities on a day-to-day basis.

Translanguaging

Translanguaging is when speakers draw from their complex language repertoire during the course of a single conversation. ELs frequently translanguage, both at school and in their home and communities. Translanguaging shifts focus from the languages themselves and centers on the observable practices bilinguals engage in, using all of their linguistic resources, to "process information, make meaning, and convey it to others" (Orellana & García, 2014, p. 386). Translanguaging in the classroom means that more than one language is used systematically in a single learning activity, usually for different communicative functions. The use of the verb form *to language* (e.g., *languaging* or *translanguaging*) reflects an understanding of language as a dynamic communicative practice and acknowledges that languages are not distinct in the mind but rather part of an integrated linguistic system (García, Johnson et al., 2017).

"One of the best ways to understand translanguaging is to see and hear it in action. Many teachers have 'aha moments' when they stop and listen to the ways students use language in their classrooms. For example, two students negotiate in Spanish over a math problem posed to them in English. One student with more experience in English quietly explains the directions to a newly arrived student from China. A group of students joke with one another using word play and English/Spanish puns. Once you take up this new lens for observing your bilingual students, you will notice new and exciting things about the way they language, which can guide the ways you plan, teach, assess, and advocate for their needs." (García, Johnson et al., 2017, p. 1)

Translanguaging Pedagogy

Translanguaging pedagogy describes an approach whereby teachers build bridges between translanguaging practices and the language practices expected in formal school settings. Bilingualism is the norm in translanguaging classrooms—regardless of whether the official language of instruction is English. Monolingual teachers can embrace translanguaging in their classroom as well—it is not necessary to speak any of the L1s of your students. Adopting this approach involves leveraging bilingual students' and ELs' authentic language practices (not always considered desirable in academic settings) to support them in meeting official content and language standards at school. Situating translanguaging as a communicative accomplishment and mobilizing it to achieve targeted learning objectives takes conscious effort on the part of educators. It means looking for opportunities in the classroom for students to utilize all the languages in their toolkit to

- express and comprehend meaning,
- explore topics from multiple perspectives,
- compare those topics across cultures, and
- write and speak for different audiences.

Bilingual students have the ability to draw on more than one linguistic and cultural perspective to explore a topic. They inhabit multiple worlds, so they possess a unique capacity to see multiple sides of an issue (García, Johnson et al., 2017). This is an asset. Harness it to benefit learning for everyone in the classroom. Translanguaging supports ELs in maneuvering cognitively demanding content in creative and critical ways. They are not limited to what they can express and comprehend in English. All students in the class benefit from sharing different learning strategies and negotiating among different perspectives.

Watch how Andy Brown, a Grade 5 English as a second language teacher in Queens, New York, uses translanguaging to support mathematics learning in the classroom: www.youtube.com/watch?v=O6DBPbDT_GE

If you heard students translanguaging in your classroom, would your immediate reaction be positive or negative? Think about the situation from an asset-based perspective—is there a way to extend students' translanguaging practices to make connections to the curriculum? If so, how? If not, why not?

Using Home Language to Actively Engage Learners With Relevant and Meaningful Content

Active engagement with literacy is a primary determinant of achievement at school. Extensive evidence confirms that literacy engagement is fundamental to students' success and is an even greater determinant of academic achievement than socioeconomic status (Cummins et al., 2012). This makes sense when we consider that academic language is predominantly found in books and curriculum materials rather than in everyday conversation. Students do not encounter the patterns and structures of academic language in day-to-day conversation. Even the language spoken by teachers in the classroom is generally more social than academic in register. The only way to acquire the language of school-based literacy is through engagement with literacy itself.

The challenge for teachers is to actively engage ELs in reading and writing in a language the students cannot fully access. The use of L1 helps students grapple with complex academic language; they can transfer conceptual knowledge from their L1 to English and clarify meaning by accessing equivalences in their L1.

 "Schools need to find ways of ensuring that all students, not just those whose language practices align with those used in school, understand challenging content and texts." (García, Johnson et al., 2017, p. 8)

Often, ELs are not given a chance to work with complex texts because of their English language proficiency. The intention behind this is to prevent failure, but what actually happens is that they are prevented from understanding how language works in academic texts. Simplified texts, often given to ELs, do not provide any idea of what academic language sounds like or how it works. If students are not given opportunities to develop the lexical and grammatical resources they need to engage in academic discourse, they are unlikely to be able to communicate and comprehend complex ideas and information at school. Abundant access to a variety of print-based resources, including dual-language books, provides ELs with crucial opportunities to develop their vocabulary knowledge and strengthen their reading comprehension skills.

 Record samples of dialogue between you and one of your ELs when you are working on an academic task in the classroom and when you are having a casual conversation outside of class. What differences do you notice? Does the student have trouble understanding any of the language in the classroom? What do you do to help the student fully understand the content and/or instructions in the classroom? How could you support them more effectively?

Instructional Strategies That Use Home Language to Promote Literacy Engagement

Cummins et al. (2012) identify four instructional dimensions that, when embraced and put into practice by teachers, become critical components of literacy engagement and hence academic achievement (particularly for those from socially marginalized backgrounds):

1. Scaffold students' capacity to comprehend and use academic language using specific instructional strategies (e.g., development of learning strategies, use of visual/graphic organizers, enabling students to use their L1 [e.g., through discussion, bilingual dictionary use, or L1 digital or text resources]).

2. Connect instruction to students' lives by activating their background knowledge, which is often encoded in their L1.

3. Enable students to complete challenging academic work that showcases their literacy and language accomplishments (in both L1 and L2) and affirms their academic, linguistic, and cultural identities.

4. Explicitly develop and extend students' awareness and control of language across the curriculum (e.g., encourage students to compare L1 and L2; break down academic language into chunks).

These instructional strategies are suitable for both English as a second language (ESL) and mixed student groups (i.e., ELs and native English speakers).

Juicy Sentences (All levels)

The juicy sentence is a strategy developed by Fillmore (Fillmore & Fillmore, 2012) that addresses how to assist ELs in accessing a complex text, though it has been used successfully with non-ELs as well. Before delivering a lesson that uses an academic text, identify and record a sentence (or short passage) that may be difficult for students. Choose a suitably complex excerpt—one that contains key vocabulary, an interesting grammatical structure, or linguistic features that align with grade-level language standards. It should be a selection that communicates an important part of the reading. After reading the text in full (i.e., an exemplar, chapter, or class read aloud), engage students in an instructional conversation about the language in your chosen sentence (i.e., draw explicit attention to the ways in which meaning relates to words, phrases, or clauses in the text). The example I use here is from Frederick Douglass's *Narrative of the Life of Frederick Douglass an American Slave, Written by Himself*, included as a reading in the Common Core State Standards for English Language Arts & Literacy in History/Social Studies, Science, and Technical Subjects for Grades 6–8 Appendix, "Text Exemplars and Sample Performance Tasks" (www.corestandards.org/assets /Appendix_B.pdf; National Governors Association Center for Best Practices & Council of Chief State School Officers, 2010).

> I am strongly tempted to give the names of two or three of those little boys, as a testimonial of the gratitude and affection I bear them; but prudence forbids;—not that it would injure me, but it might embarrass them; for it is almost an unpardonable offence to teach slaves to read in this Christian country. (p. 91)

Ask open-ended questions to get the discussion started. For example:

- What do you think this sentence means?

Prompts:

- How does Douglass feel about the young boys?

- What did the boys help Douglass learn how to do?

Students discuss with a partner, ELs can use their L1. Ask students to share their thoughts with the class (in English). Discuss vocabulary (e.g., what does the word *for* mean in this context? What is an equivalent? [I.e., *because.*] Ask ELs to share an equivalent in their L1). Talk about the use of context clues to help deduce meaning. Guide students into a discussion of how the sentence relates to the rest of the text.

Ask students what they notice about the sentence. This generally requires modeling, but after several examples over time, students are generally able to do the noticing independently. This work is guided by the grade-level language standards and may involve tasks like circling verbs and discussing tense (e.g., use of modals *would/might* to express possibility in this example), prefixes or suffixes and discussing meanings (e.g., *un*pardonable—discuss that *un–* is a prefix meaning *not*), or punctuation and discussing purpose (e.g., semicolons used to join two or more related sentences can be used in place of a period), and so on.

Options

- Discuss why the author might have chosen to use certain structures or included certain information.

- Break the sentence down into parts and identify the information conveyed in each.

- Challenge students to rewrite the sentence in their own words, using the same structure the author used.

Fillmore and Fillmore (2012) note that 15–20 minutes spent discussing the language in just one sentence on a regular basis will "help students learn to unpack the information so tightly packed into academic texts and, in doing so, gradually internalize an awareness of the relation between specific linguistic patterns and the functions they serve in texts" (p. 69). Aim to work with a juicy sentence at least once a week (every day or every other day is even better). Noticing how language is used in text is an important first step in navigating the complexities of academic language.

This activity is beneficial for all students and can be done as a whole class activity with both ESL and mixed student groups.

For other resources, visit:

- The Standards Institute: ideas on how to use juicy sentences in the classroom, handouts for students, and prep sheets for teachers (www.standardsinstitutes.org/sites/default/files/material/summer16_ela_grades _p-3_day_3_handout_-_complex_texts.pdf)

- "Classroom Example of Teaching Complex Text Butterfly HD": kindergarten (youtube.com/watch?v=Cu_1u7Y7gSM)

- "5th Grade Juicy Sentence": video showing teachers doing juicy sentences in the classroom (youtu.be/XGBunYg5Iuc)

- Fillmore and Fillmore's (2012) article "What Does Text Complexity Mean for English Learners and Language Minority Students?": an in-depth discussion and exemplar of how teachers can help ELs grapple with academic language (ell.stanford.edu/sites/default/files/pdf/academic-papers/06-LWF CJF Text Complexity FINAL_0.pdf)

Using Home Language to Facilitate Differentiated Learning

Differentiated instruction (DI) is an instructional model that provides multiple pathways to learning and offers differing challenges to a diverse student population group (TESOL International Association, 2018). DI does not mean that teachers reduce the complexity of instructional objectives but instead scaffold instruction for student success (Tomlinson, 2014). L1 can serve as a vital scaffold for English language, literacy, and content learning. More cognitively demanding tasks, like literacy, problem-solving, and abstract thinking involve skills and knowledge that are common across languages. The interdependence of languages in the mind means that students can use what they know in their L1 to scaffold their learning in English. In addition to acting as a support to ELs, L1 provides those who have transitioned to fluent English proficient (i.e., former ELs who have met required English proficiency benchmarks, had language supports removed, and are now expected to participate equally in the school's regular instructional program) with opportunities in the English-medium classroom to draw on all their language resources in ways that can help to compensate for an absence of formal language support. The amount of L1 that is used in the classroom can be adjusted based on the demands of the task and an individual learner's English language proficiency levels, needs, and goals. Including L1 in differentiated instruction can make the difference between ELs actively participating in age- and cognitively appropriate learning or being relegated to simplified tasks that fail to equip them with the tools they need to succeed at school.

Wordless Books

Wordless picture books, most useful for Grades K–6, tell a story through images alone and are a fun and powerful tool that can be used to scaffold both oral and written skills in any language. Skills you can teach using wordless books include predicting, sequencing (beginning, middle, end), inferencing, creative writing, writing dialogue, reading confidence, and connecting to background knowledge. They can also be used to teach and practice subject-specific and academic vocabulary in English and L1. Because of their versatility, activities using wordless books can be easily differentiated based on individual student needs and learning objectives.

These books level the playing field for many students who are able to get at the story without having to decode words. There are many high-quality wordless books—a simple Google search will yield numerous options. In addition to choosing books that are appropriate for your grade level and/or content area, be sure to include ones that represent people of diverse racial and cultural backgrounds. Here are a few recommendations organized by grade ranges, though most wordless books can be used across grade levels.

Grades K–2

- *Flashlight* (Lizi Boyd): A flashlight reveals all the things that happen at night.

- *El Globito Rojo* (Iela Mari): Readers follow a balloon and watch it transform.

- *The Lion and the Mouse* (Jerry Pinkney): An unlikely pair learns that no act of kindness is ever wasted.

Grades 3–5

- *Mirror* (Jeannie Baker): Readers explore the differences and similarities of two boys—one living in Morocco, the other in Australia.

- *Chalk* (Bill Thompson): Three children find a seemingly magic bag of chalk that makes their drawings come to life.

- *Pool* (Jihyeon Lee): Two shy children meet at a very crowded pool.

Grade 6

- *Flotsam* (David Wiesner): A young boy goes to the beach to learn about marine life and makes an unexpected discovery.

- *The Arrival* (Shaun Tan): An immigrant father embarks on a journey in search of a better life for his family as told through an imaginary world.

Activities Using Wordless Books and L1

These wordless book activities can be implemented with both ESL and mixed student groups.

Retell (Grades K–6)

After reading a wordless book as a whole class, pair students up to retell the story in their own words. If possible, partner same-L1 students together and invite them to retell the story using their L1 or a combination of L1 and English. Alternatively, ELs can work with a bilingual teacher or volunteer or use an online translator to tell the story in their L1 and translate it into English.

Introduce sequencing vocabulary like *first, second, next, then*; *before/after*; *during*; *meanwhile*; *eventually*; *earlier/later*; *previously*, and so on. Assist ELs in finding L1 equivalents and/or ask them to share any they already know. This vocabulary can be added to the multilingual word wall or recorded in students' bilingual dictionaries.

***Storytelling* (Grades K–6)**

If you want to encourage creativity, skip the whole class reading and go right to having students tell a story orally to a partner. Give each set of partners a different wordless book and have them practice telling their oral story a few times. Then have pairs tell their story to the rest of class. This activity can be customized to your student group, proficiency levels, and/or learning objective. Consider pairing up an EL with a monolingual English student to facilitate a bilingual retelling of the story. Or pair up same-L1 peers to translanguage.

⭐ *Jigsaw* (Grades K–6)

Cut out each page from the book, black out page numbers, and distribute one to each student (if the pages are double-sided, you will need an additional copy of the book or photocopies of pages so that each student has a single page from the story). Ask students to work together to put the story in order. As they work to sequence the story, to develop inferencing skills, ask specific questions about the decisions they are making related to the story's plot and characters. (E.g., "Why do you think he is doing that?", "Why do you think that object is there?") Ask ELs to describe actions or objects in the story in their L1.

Once students have sequenced their pages and retold their version of the story, read the actual book as a whole class and compare students' predictions to the original. Focus on teaching and practicing key vocabulary (e.g., sequencing, predicting, focal content words). Using the images from the book, invite ELs to share any L1 equivalents they know for the key vocabulary. Add any key vocabulary to the word wall (including L1 equivalents).

⭐ *Wordless Book Poetry* (Grades 2–6)

Ask students to write words or phrases to describe the story on sticky notes. Encourage ELs to use a combination of L1 and English. This activity can be less intimidating for many students than being tasked with writing complete sentences. Prompt students, if needed, by asking questions about the story (E.g., "What do you see?", "What is happening?", "How does that character feel?") Once students have made it through the book, ask them to lay out their sticky notes so they can see them all at once. Have them rearrange the words and phrases to create a poem and share their poems with the class.

⭐ *Creative Writing* (Grades 2–6)

Have students add text to accompany each page of the story using key vocabulary discussed during a prior oral retelling of the story. Model adding text to the first one or two pages and elicit an EL's help in translating your English text into a language other than English to encourage dual-language writing. Modify the activity for younger grades or for older students who are using a longer or more complex book, like *The Arrival* by Shaun Tan, by having students write text for just one or two pages. Alternatively, students can practice writing dialogue by adding speech bubbles to the characters in the story. Again, depending on the composition of your student group, facilitate the creation of dual-language texts by pairing same-L1 pairs or an EL with a monolingual English peer. Dialogue can include translanguaging!

Using Home Language to Promote the Use of Learning Strategies and Critical Thinking

Students are making connections between their L1 and English every day in the classroom regardless of whether it is acknowledged or permitted by the teacher. Learning efficiencies can be gained by explicitly drawing attention to the similarities and differences between languages and helping students to apply the learning strategies they are likely already using in effective ways (Cummins, 2007a). Following, I identify specific types of learning strategies and describe how L1 can be used to apply those strategies in ways that optimize student learning.

- *Metacognitive and metalinguistic strategies* (e.g., noticing of different language features and how they are used, self-monitoring comprehension and production, selective attention, strategies of visualizing, organizational planning) transfer across languages. Students can draw on what they know in their L1 (e.g., cognates, concepts) and transfer that to their new language learning. Teachers can facilitate this transfer by engaging students in activities that create space for students to make connections between what they are learning in class and what they know in their L1—from linguistic structures (e.g., "How would you say this sentence in Mandarin?", "Where do adjectives go in Arabic—before or after the noun?", "I don't know that either, let's use Google Translate and compare") to conceptual knowledge (e.g., "Is there a word for that in Spanish?", "Is there an expression like that in Tagalog?", "How is it the same as or different from the English version?")

- *Cognitive strategies* (i.e., critical thinking that involves deliberate use of language to enhance learning) and related tasks (e.g., repetition, note-taking, guessing meaning from context, extending prior knowledge) can be coordinated across languages. Taking notes using L1 or a combination of L1 and English can be more efficient than note-taking in English alone, allowing students more time to focus on the auditory input; prewriting in the L1 before completing a writing assignment in English often produces more complex writing in English; accessing conceptual knowledge encoded in the L1 to learn content material in English helps students to keep up with the curriculum regardless of their English language proficiency. These are all examples of cognitive strategies that can be reinforced across all the languages in a student's repertoire.

- *Social/affective strategies* (i.e., strategies involving factors such as emotions and attitudes) also benefit from explicit inclusion of L1 (e.g., cooperating with others, empathizing, asking clarification questions, self-talk). As already mentioned, being able to access L1 in the classroom can lead to lower anxiety levels and a more emotionally positive learning experience. If students know that they can use all of the languages in their toolkit to grapple with content and communicate clearly with peers and teachers, they will feel more comfortable and prepared to engage in the social behaviors necessary to learn language. Affective strategies involving L1 can result in greater control of feelings and related behaviors that impact learning.

Unfortunately, it is not uncommon to see ELs being kept busy and quiet in the classroom with endless worksheets while their classmates exercise higher order thinking skills, such as inquiry-based learning, creative work, and generating new knowledge. "If they can't do it in English, then they aren't ready to do it" is an unfortunately persistent misconception. Learning strategies that explicitly draw on L1 allow students to guide and plan their learning more efficiently and effectively, engage in critical thinking with greater ease, and grapple with challenging content alongside peers.

Using Home Language to Promote Students' Self-Regulated Learning

L1 use has been shown to enhance learning efficiency and foster autonomy in students (Levine, 2013). Being able to draw on prior knowledge and L1 resources often means students rely less on teachers exclusively to help them complete tasks. This increased autonomy can lead to greater confidence and self-reliance in the classroom. When ELs are permitted to draw on all their cognitive and linguistic resources, they are better able to take ownership of their learning. They have the tools to be able to tackle tasks more independently and steer their own course in accomplishing them.

Using L1 as a scaffold for greater autonomy and academic engagement creates active participants rather than passive recipients in the learning process. This often results in deeper understanding, more efficient appropriation of concepts and key vocabulary, and, importantly, a learning environment with greater emotional positivity overall. Students who have access to all their resources for learning are better equipped to cope with the challenges of learning curricular content and a new language simultaneously. With the support of their L1 and prior knowledge, students can maintain high expectations for themselves and teachers can mirror those same expectations back.

Principle 4: Adapt Lesson Delivery as Needed

This principle is directly relevant to the discussion in Chapter 2 on spontaneous L1 moments that arise as a natural part of responsive teaching (pp. 33–34). Responsive teaching means evaluating what students know, what they do not know, and how well they are grappling with a given task as it is happening. L1 is a valuable pedagogical tool that teachers can utilize to effectively support students in real time as they work through tasks. Based on learner responses, L1 may be used to aid comprehension of auditory and written input, scaffold learning, and/or provide opportunities for students to demonstrate learning. The four factors described in Chapter 2 (efficiency, learning, real-world relevance, social justice) will help you to make in-the-moment decisions about L1 use, as will the following Practice suggestions, which have been adapted from TESOL's 6 Principles to include L1.

10–2 Activities (All levels)
TESOL International Association (2018) suggests using a structure like 10–2 activities, where teachers interrupt their oral output every 10 minutes to provide students with 2-minute opportunities to interact with the new learning. ELs expend extra effort comprehending auditory input while they are simultaneously concentrating on the content of what is being said. If they are given intermittent opportunities to interact with others about the input (e.g., think, pair, share; turn and talk; sketch and share), they achieve deeper understanding and greater retention of the material.

These opportunities to consolidate learning are enhanced if students can use their L1 to verify their understanding of what they heard in English with same-L1 peers. Sometimes, the barriers to comprehension that an EL experiences when listening to the teacher (e.g., unfamiliar vocabulary, complex language structures), may persist if they are restricted to using English only when interacting with peers. L1 use here allows students to make explicit connections to prior knowledge and keep up with the content of the lesson. They stay abreast of the curriculum regardless of their language proficiency.

These 2-minute breaks also provide an opportunity for teachers to check comprehension and provide necessary support; for example, if a student does not share an L1 with any in-class peers, the teacher can take this time to clarify content with the student by providing alternate modes of input (e.g., visual aids, simplified language, or L1 using a machine translator).

⭐ ***Quick Comprehension Checks*** (**All levels**)
Group response techniques are a useful gauge of how students are faring in the midst of a lesson. Comprehension checks can be as simple as eliciting a thumbs up/thumbs down; response boards (dry erase boards used for individual responses); stoplight (three cut circles for each student to indicate green for good to go, yellow for need more practice, or red for stop and reteach); or a digital student response system like Poll Everywhere (www.polleverywhere.com/k12-student-response-system).

In some cases, individual response checks may be more appropriate, particularly in mixed student groups where ELs are integrated among dominant language peers. Especially for newcomers, introverts, or others who hesitate to speak up, privately arranging a discrete response technique that a student can utilize without attracting undue attention to themselves will often mean students more readily seek help when they need it. Some covert individual responses include a headshake, placing an object (e.g., a particular eraser or pencil case) on the desk in front of them, or a hand on the forehead.

⭐ ***Adapt the Product of the Learning Task*** (**All levels**)
Providing equitable access to education for ELs involves adapting projects, group tasks, assignments, presentations, demonstrations, tests, and so on to allow students with emergent English and developing skills to demonstrate learning and curriculum knowledge. An English-only learning space often means that ELs are limited in their ability to communicate what they have learned. This makes it nearly impossible for teachers to differentiate between what students know and can do and what they know and can do through English.

Create bilingual culminating projects and presentations that can be understood by a diverse, multilingual audience. Have students create bilingual products across a variety of genres (e.g., oral presentations, written texts, dramatic play, video, posters) and rationalize their language choices.

Provide different language options for tasks. Examples:

- A handout included with a group discussion activity gives three options: *(a) Discuss in English, record your answers in English; (b) Discuss in English and Mandarin, record your answers in English; (c) Discuss in English and Mandarin, record your answers in English and Mandarin (e.g., write down a key English word or phrase and expand on it in Mandarin).*

- Instructions for a written response to class reading include the statement: *You can make notes in English, your L1, or both, regardless of the written language of the text.*

In the case where students write down their answers in a language other than English, teachers can ask students to orally explain their answers in English or use a machine translation tool to facilitate assessment. Machine translators do not provide perfect translations every time but they are accurate enough to allow the teacher to assess the quality of the content of a response.

Principle 5: Monitor and Assess Student Language Development

The practices associated with this principle include monitoring students' learning and providing ongoing, effective feedback, as well as designing varied and valid assessments and supports to assess learning. L1 has a crucial role to play in facilitating these practices. First, the value of positive or corrective feedback is limited if the student receiving the feedback has no or only partial understanding of what is being communicated (either orally or in writing). Discussing the feedback or confirming comprehension using the students' L1 with the help of a same-L1 peer or machine translator means the student acquires a clear understanding and can then use the feedback constructively going forward.

Second, assessments that restrict ELs to using English only are compromised in both their validity and fairness. The only truly equitable way of assessing ELs is to permit them to use their entire linguistic repertoire to demonstrate knowledge and competency. It is imperative to ensure that a student's general linguistic performance (i.e., their use of language to express complex thoughts—e.g., persuade, explain, critique) and their specific language performance (i.e., their use of a specific language—e.g., Mandarin, English, Spanish) are not conflated (García, Johnson et al., 2017). Students may have appropriated a concept in the course of classroom learning but be unable to orally communicate that knowledge in English.

This has important implications for assessment. How can we accurately and fairly assess an EL's content learning if they are restricted to using English only to communicate? Their language proficiency becomes the determining factor in any evaluation of their learning; every assessment becomes an assessment of language (American Educational Research Association et al., 2014). The inclusion of L1 corrects this very serious flaw in assessment for linguistically diverse students. L1 makes it possible to differentiate what a student knows and can do using their entire linguistic repertoire from what they are able to demonstrate using only English.

 Otheguy et al. (2015) discuss the differences in school assessment for bilingual vs. monolingual students: "In schools in general, but especially during testing, bilingual students, to their great disadvantage, are kept from using their entire language repertoires, are compelled to suppress a big part of their idiolect; are not allowed to translanguage. In contrast, monolingual students, to their great advantage, are forced to suppress only a small fraction of their idiolect (the part that is interpersonally inappropriate); are regularly allowed to translanguage. Both types of students are asked to be part of a teaching and testing game that each ends up playing under different rules. It is small wonder that the monolingual side usually comes out on top." (pp. 300–301)

García, Johnson et al. (2017) provide a translanguaging design for assessment, which gathers information across a student's language repertoire to evaluate what they know and can do with content and language relative to standards, objectives, and culminating projects. They suggest that teachers observe students' performance on various instructional tasks leading up to and including final projects based on two questions:

1. Is the student using all the features of his or her language repertoire and/or using language-specific features?

2. Is the student performing independently, with moderate assistance from other people or other resources, or is the performance emergent? (García, Johnson et al., 2017, p. 86).

These framing questions help to separate language proficiency from a student's knowledge and skills across the curriculum. Although we often think of assessments as fixed and inflexible, teachers can adjust both formative and summative assessment instruments to capture what students can do with two (or more) languages independently as well as what they can do using their entire linguistic reserve. Not only does this lead to a more accurate appraisal of students' capacities and understandings, but also allows teachers to more clearly assess the specific challenges students are encountering (e.g., content, a particular higher order thinking skill, English proficiency) and take targeted steps (e.g., language supports, learning scaffolds) to transform their progress. See Appendix F for a student (plurilingual) performance by task template that will help you to separate students' demonstrated competencies across languages vs what they are able to do using only English or only their L1.

⭐ *Differentiating Objectives: A Sample Unit Plan* (Grades 9–12)
Divide content objectives for a particular lesson or unit plan into "objectives across languages" and "language-specific objectives." If you do not speak the L1(s) of your students, you can use a machine translation tool to check L1 equivalents. Following is a simplified sample unit plan that demonstrates how to design more valid and equitable assessment for ELs. This plan is designed for a mixed student group with Spanish-L1 ELs, bilingual students, and monolingual native English speakers.

Unit Plan Title: The Times Are A-Changing*

Content Area: Social Studies (History/Geography/Civics)

Grade Levels: 9–12

Essential Questions

- What events and ideas have catalyzed social change over time?
- What circumstances motivate people to challenge power and authority?
- Who holds power in our society?

Unit Guiding Questions

- How might the historical narrative change based on who is telling it? (i.e., Who writes the stories? Who benefits from the stories? Who loses? Who is missing from the stories?)

(continued on the next page)

Unit Guiding Questions *(continued)*

- What did Rep. John Lewis mean when he said "Get in good trouble, necessary trouble"?
- How can civil disobedience bring about change?
- What makes an act of civil disobedience effective?
- How do geographic representations (over time) illuminate the inequitable distribution of resources and/or systemic racism?

Fundamental Geographical and Historical Concepts: Continuity and change; power and governance; systems and structures; interactions and interdependence; distribution of resources; primary/secondary sources; historical interpretation/narrative

Related Concepts Addressed in this Unit: Human and natural patterns, civic rights and responsibilities; cause and effect; conflict and cooperation; social/political/cultural spaces; ideology; power relations; justice; democracy

LITERACY**

Grades 9–10	Grades 11–12
CCSS.ELA-LITERACY.RH.9-10.1	CCSS.ELA-LITERACY.RH.11-12.1
CCSS.ELA-LITERACY.RH.9-10.2	CCSS.ELA-LITERACY.RH.11-12.2
CCSS.ELA-LITERACY.WHST.9-10.1	CCSS.ELA-LITERACY.WHST.11-12.2
CCSS.ELA-LITERACY.WHST.9-10.6	CCSS.ELA-LITERACY.WHST.11-12.6

Content & Language Objectives

Students will gather information about historical movements for civil rights and civil liberties over the past 150 years and examine how individuals and groups have advanced social justice by pushing back against structures of power and authority.

Teams will create a 10-minute multimedia presentation documenting the historical and contemporary efforts of one focal group's fight to achieve civil rights and civil liberties for all in the United States or another country of choice.

Students will gather data, make inferences, and draw conclusions from maps and demographic data representing patterns of human movement (e.g., African American migration from 1910–1920, urban/suburban development under the New Deal).

Students will create a poster map using Padlet (www.padlet.com) where they will place articles, photos, and other artifacts to represent a chosen pattern of migration and underlying impetus.

Objectives Across Languages

Students will be able to

- evaluate primary and secondary sources.
- critically analyze and interpret data.
- develop arguments based on evidence from a variety of sources.
- organize and synthesize complex ideas, concepts, and information using multiple modes (e.g., text, images, video).
- collaborate in a small group to generate a multimedia presentation based on information gathered and analyzed from multiple sources.
- integrate different dialects or languages other than English (where appropriate) by choosing certain words, phrases, or expressions to better represent point of view.

Language-Specific Objectives

Students will be able to

- demonstrate the ability to apply and comprehend critical language in English (e.g., human rights, civil disobedience, immigration, discrimination, civic engagement, equity, equality, protest) and equivalents in L1 (for ELs).
- in English and Spanish, use signal words to argue a point (e.g., contend/*contender*, assert/*afirmar*, posit/*proponer*, advocate/*abogar por*, perceive/*percibir*, defend/*defender*).
- in English and Spanish, use sequencing words or phrases to order events (e.g., prior to/*anterior a eso*, subsequently/*con posterioridad*, consequently/*por consiguiente*, in advance of/*en avance de*, initially/*inicialmente*).

(continued on the next page)

Culminating Project

In small groups, students will create and present a multimedia project based on information gathered, summarized, and analyzed from primary and secondary sources. Individually, students will create a poster map on Padlet representing their interpretation of data collected from maps and demographic information, critically representing a pattern of human migration resulting from social change.

Other Assessment

Student Self-Assessment***
Peer Assessment

Texts and/or Resources

In English

- Black Migration to the North 1910–1920 (www.youtube.com/watch?v=sUKTT7Yd4eA)
- Civil Rights and Hispanics in Texas (www.youtube.com/watch?v=dzfdINufpSE)
- Housing segregation and redlining in America: A short history (www.youtube.com/watch?v=O5FBJyqfoLM)
- King, Martin Luther, Jr. (1963). *I Have a Dream: Writings and Speeches that Changed the World* (www.dhs.gov/office-civil-rights-and-civil-liberties)
- Latino Civil Rights Timeline, 1903 to 2006 (www.tolerance.org/classroom-resources/tolerance-lessons/latino-civil-rights-timeline-1903-to-2006)
- J. W. Loewen, *Lies My Teacher Told Me* (2007; Chapters 5 and 6)
- B. Obama (2004). *Speech to the Democratic National Convention* (www.washingtonpost.com/wp-dyn/articles/A19751-2004Jul27.html)
- National Museum of African American History & Cultures. *The Historical Legacy of Juneteeth* (nmaahc.si.edu/blog-post/historical-legacy-juneteenth)
- Close Reading of a Primary Document (teachinghistory.org/best-practices/examples-of-historical-thinking/19528)
- Gettysburg Address (www.abrahamlincolnonline.org/lincoln/speeches/gettysburg.htm)
- Classroom poster outlining historical thinking; can register for a free account (sheg.stanford.edu/historical-thinking-chart)
- National Geographic map search (www.nationalgeographic.org/map/)

In Spanish

- T. Morlock (2017), *El Movimiento Por Los Derechos Civiles de Los Mexicoamericanos*
- Movimiento Chicano [Chicano Movement] (www.brown.edu/Research/Coachella/chicano_es.html)
- Un recorrido por el movimiento de derechos civiles en Estados Unidos [A Tour of the Civil Rights Movement in the United States] (www.youtube.com/watch?v=DMhUtW84VPI)
- Google Maps (en español) [in Spanish] (www.google.com/maps/?hl=es)
- Discurso de Gettysburg [Gettysburg Address] (www.youtube.com/watch?v=WXZGlRTeUss)
- Tengo un sueño, discurso completo de Martin Luther King [I Have a Dream, full speech by Martin Luther King] (www.univision.com/noticias/noticias-de-eeuu/i-have-a-dream-discurso-completo-de-martin-luther-king)

Note: Setting your search engine homepage to Spanish by selecting "Settings > Languages > Spanish" under the search bar will generate a "*Traducir esta página*/Translate this page" option for any webpage that comes up in a site search. This works when the browser is set to any language other than English.

---

*See Appendix D for a blank plurilingual unit planning template.

**Common Core State Standards Initiative. (2020). *English language arts standards, history/social studies: Grade 9–10*. http://www.corestandards.org/ELA-Literacy/RH/9-10/; *Grade 11–12*. http://www.corestandards.org/ELA-Literacy/RH/11-12/

***See Appendixes G.1 and G.2 for student assessment templates.

Principle 6: Engage and Collaborate Within a Community of Practice

A community of practice is made up of individuals who share a profession and engage with each other in collectively learning more about that profession (TESOL International Association, 2018). As our classrooms become increasingly diverse, it becomes more imperative that teachers work collaboratively with others who specialize in areas outside of their own skill set to inform their teaching and add to their cache of teaching techniques. This might mean collaborating with teachers in special education, science and math, literacy, and ESL/English language development. Bilingual teachers, in particular, can be rich sources of knowledge. Colleagues who teach in bilingual or dual-language programs or who share the same linguistic or cultural background of our students are potential resources for helping us to better understand the structures of students' L1s and the cultures from which our students come (TESOL International Association, 2018). Although it has been emphasized throughout this book that teachers do not need to speak the L1s of their students to incorporate those L1s into classroom learning, making an effort to actively accumulate knowledge about students' diverse languages and cultural backgrounds can help teachers recognize and leverage those assets as opportunities to enrich and extend school-based learning for everyone, rather than focus on the challenges that come from attempting to make diverse students fit into a narrow, exclusionary curriculum.

Packed schedules mean that this kind of collaboration or coplanning among teachers often takes place informally, at lunch, during break times, or before or after school. School administrators have a role to play in arranging scheduling in such a way that allows teachers to come together in collaborative professional learning teams to share knowledge and teaching tools. Some professional development time could be allotted to developing personal learning networks and collaborating within communities of practice. As discussed in the introduction to this book, working toward more effective and equitable instruction for ELs involves incorporating accountability for ELs more broadly throughout schools and school districts. This means establishing communities of practice within the school and across schools—motivated by an understanding that everyone is responsible for the success of ELs—not exclusively EL teachers and EL department staff.

Principle 6 also includes the use of reflective practice as an essential component of engaging within a community of practice. TESOL International Association (2018) notes that this involves examining our assumptions of everyday practice and evaluating them; as Larrivee (2000) articulates, "Unless teachers develop the practice of critical reflection, they stay trapped in unexamined judgments, interpretations, assumptions, and expectations. Approaching teaching as a reflective practitioner involves fusing personal beliefs and values into a professional identity" (p. 293). The assumptions and knowledge presented in Chapter 1 can be utilized to support this work. Sharing knowledge, experiences, and practical tools with colleagues increases professional competency and capacity to enact equitable instruction for all students.

Examining and naming our assumptions, judgements, and expectations related to diverse students is a crucial part of reflecting on practice and enacting more equitable instruction. Harvard University's Project Implicit (implicit.harvard.edu /implicit) has a variety of Implicit Association Tests designed to measure an individual's implicit biases—attitudes and beliefs that people may be unwilling or unable to report. This test can be taken online by anyone and can reveal if you have an implicit attitude that you did not know about.

Chapter 3 Review

TESOL's 6 Principles (TESOL International Association, 2018) provide a concise set of guidelines that any teacher of ELs can use to inform and support teaching practices that optimally serve these students. This chapter described how the use of L1 can complement the implementation of The 6 Principles into your practice.

Principle 1: Know Your Learners. L1 facilitates learning about our students; their backgrounds, prior knowledge, and individual learning needs. L1 use transforms the extent to which parents and caregivers with limited to no English can be involved in their child's education. Crucial connections can be made between home literacies and school-based literacies. Bilingual teaching strategies reinforce to students and families that reading, writing, and interacting in any language develops literacy and intellectual growth.

Principle 2: Create Conditions for Language Learning. An inclusive and emotionally positive learning environment recognizes that language is inextricable from a student's identity. By validating a student's L1 as legitimate at school and harnessing it as a valuable resource for learning, we create safe classroom spaces where students can meet high expectations because they have access to the tools they need to achieve.

Principle 3: Design High-Quality Lessons for Language Development. Incorporating L1s into lesson planning and delivery assures clear communication of lesson instructions and outcomes; takes advantage of the interdependence of languages in the mind to maximize comprehensible input; promotes authentic language use by acknowledging and incorporating translanguaging into instruction as a legitimate and sophisticated linguistic practice; provides access to cognitively challenging texts and promotes active literacy engagement; aids in differentiated instruction; achieves learning efficiencies and bolsters critical thinking; and fosters greater self-reliance and autonomy.

Principle 4: Adapt Lesson Delivery as Needed. Inviting students' L1s into the learning process opens up a treasure trove of instructional strategies that can be used to respond to in-the-moment needs in ways that optimally support students in accomplishing objectives.

Principle 5: Monitor and Assess Student Language Development. L1 has a pivotal role to play in assessment. Not only does it ensure that students clearly understand feedback so that they can use it constructively, it is indispensable to fair and valid assessment. L1 allows teachers to differentiate between students' language proficiency and their competencies and knowledge. This differentiation provides valuable insight into specific areas of difficulty for students and, importantly, separates English language proficiency from what a student knows and can do.

Principle 6: Engage and Collaborate Within a Community of Practice. Gaining knowledge about students' languages and cultural background by collaborating with other teachers within a community of practice is an important component of professional growth, as is critical reflection on practice, which involves examining our assumptions, interpretations, and expectations in relation to students of diverse backgrounds.

CHAPTER 4

MOVING TOWARD A
MORE EQUITABLE FUTURE

The shift from deficit to asset-based perspectives produces shifts in how we define English learners' (ELs) contributions and successes at school. When we are more aware of the power differentials at play within our classroom walls and in broader society, we are more apt to recognize and applaud "the complex ways in which our students are able to navigate monolingual, 'standard' English-centric educational spaces and for the powerful contributions they make to their communities and families as cultural brokers" (Pérez & Saavedra, 2017, p. 2).

When we view ELs as emerging bilinguals, achieving communicative feats not possible for monolinguals, we challenge deficit perspectives and focus on accomplishments rather than perceived limitations. When we let go of the traditional authoritarian role and invite students to share their unique expertise, the classroom can become a shared place of inquiry. When we understand the pivotal role of identity negotiation and maintain high expectations for our ELs, we can deliver instruction and engage in classroom interactions that communicate those expectations.

This chapter examines the standards against which we measure ELs' success in using language, contemplates course materials that more accurately reflect the diversity in our classrooms, considers potential discrepancies between language competence and language performance, and, finally, advocates for adopting a plurilingual orientation that envisions and enacts more equitable education for culturally and linguistically diverse students.

 "We should, of course, be trying to create bilinguals not native speakers of the L2. This requires a fundamental shift in how teachers need to conceptualize the L2 learning curriculum and pedagogy." (Macaro, 2010, p. 301)

The Monolingual Native Speaker Bias

The monolingual native speaker bias refers to the idea that we often take for granted that the only appropriate models of a language's use come from its "native" speakers—specifically, those who speak the standard form. Teachers, and often students themselves, aim for native-like proficiency; the models provided in the classroom are overwhelmingly those of native English speakers, and students are tested on how closely their English skills approximate speakers of standard forms of English. However, the knowledge of the additional language (L2) for most bilinguals is different than that of native speakers, and the language practices of most bilinguals are different than those of native speakers. But difference is not deficit.

Bilinguals are *multicompetent*, defined here as having knowledge of more than one language in the same mind (Cook & Wei, 2016). Multicompetence is intrinsically more complex than monolingualism. Bilinguals are not simply "two monolinguals in one" (Grosjean, 1989), so there is no reason why a person's L2 should be identical to the monolingual's home language (L1). ELs should not be seen as "deficient monolinguals" or bilinguals with "defective L2s," but as talented multicompetent language users in their own right. If we teach as though language learners will only be successful when they attain native speaker language knowledge and performance, we risk perpetually viewing ELs as "less than" their non-EL counterparts. We disregard their accomplishments in comprehending and communicating in more than one language.

"Do not see yourselves as failures always trying to be like native speakers; see yourselves as successes, achieving things as L2 users that are out of the reach of monolinguals." (Cook, 2016, p. 187)

"... Teachers, researchers, and people in general have often taken for granted that L2 learners represent a special case that can be properly judged by the standards of another group. Grammar that differs from native speakers', pronunciation that betrays where L2 users come from, and vocabulary that differs from native usage are treated as signs of L2 users' failure to become native speakers, not of their accomplishments in learning to use the L2." (Cook, 1999, pp. 194–195)

Cook (2002) defines an L2 user as a person who uses another language for any purpose at whatever level, arguing that "L2 learner" is a term that implies the person is always learning, never achieving. ELs are not monolingual native English speakers, so do you agree with Cook that they should not be expected to conform to the norms of a group to which they do not belong? In your instruction, how could you integrate a focus on these students' achievements as users of more than one language rather than their perceived deficits when compared to native English speakers?

Redefining Success

One of the potential transformational aspects of valorizing languages other than English in the classroom is that we may come closer to reconceptualizing what it means to be successful as an EL and as such, set goals for language proficiency that are more appropriate to our students. In principle, a more appropriate target for ELs would be to use English like effective L2 users, not like monolingual native English speakers. This is an inherent part of acknowledging an EL's full linguistic repertoire and all the knowledge and experience encoded within as a resource for learning. Herein lies a pivotal role for many teachers of ELs in reconceptualizing how we define the successful use of English. Admittedly, measuring students against an L2 user standard is easier said than done. There are no descriptions of what successful L2 English might be; L2 user standards are nowhere to be found in curriculum documents, and you would be hard-pressed to find a syllabus that is based on teaching English for international communication rather than for communication with native speakers.

 "L2 user-ness is not a shameful condition but rather normal, natural, and even creative. With regard to classroom practice, accepting L2 use means that pronunciation and linguistic accuracy cannot be the principal measures of success. Teachers must emphasize the many kinds of L2 use: listening to authentic texts of all kinds, reading for information and for pleasure, browsing the internet, chatting informally using social media, and so on." (Scott, 2016, p. 451)

Until minds and institutions shift from a focus on "nativeness" to a focus on intelligibility and comprehensibility, the use of a native speaker model will have to suffice as an imperfect standard. But this does not mean that the traditional power of the native speaker should not be critically interrogated by schools and teachers. Nor does it mean we should not work toward establishing L2 user norms and providing L2 user role models at school. We should reflect on whether it is appropriate to penalize bilingual students when they deviate from native speaker norms if they are functioning well in English or through a combination of English and their L1. We should consider whether intelligibility is a more appropriate goal than nativeness and recognize that intelligibility does not require an accent-free performance of the L2.

This mindset signals an important move away from seeing our ELs as failed native speakers and toward valuing their multicompetence. Instead of focusing on how closely the surface aspects of an EL's language use imitate native English speakers (e.g., grammar, pronunciation, vocabulary), we should focus on what they are able to do with their language skills, including what they accomplish using all the languages in their repertoire. García (2017) suggests that students and teachers need to "value success as performances along a bilingual continuum that is always shifting. Linguistic performances should be assessed only in relationship to the speakers' specific action and the success of its communicative intent" (p. 634).

When measuring success in using language, shift focus from how the ELs in your classroom compare to monolingual speakers of standard English and instead ask yourself whether they are able to

- communicate effectively in a variety of social settings (transmitting and comprehending intended messages in appropriate ways based on context and audience, including those that are multilingual);

- achieve academically in content areas;

- take ownership of their learning, both independently and in groups;

- use effective learning strategies;

- function in an information- and technology-based society;

- advocate for themselves;

- use critical literacy and critical thinking skills to interpret the world around them; and

- participate, to their desired extent, in social, cultural, political, and economic life.

Remember as well that just because a student is unable to demonstrate a learning objective in English, doesn't mean they lack that knowledge or skill. When considering whether a student is achieving academically, ask yourself whether the use of L1 would support them in demonstrating their knowledge. Providing access to L1 alongside English enables ELs to show their full range of competencies while simultaneously scaffolding L2 development.

⭐ Global Connections: Student Partnership Projects for the 21st Century (Grades 3–12, adult)

Global partnership projects are technology-mediated collaborations whereby students from different parts of the world connect using Web 2.0 tools to cocreate multimedia projects. Research has shown that global learning networks can promote L2 learning by providing opportunities for authentic L2 use (Skourtou et al., 2006). Students are exposed to different languages and varieties of English and learn to collaborate across geographical, cultural, and linguistic borders. ELs have the opportunity to draw on the full repertoire of their linguistic toolkits. They can showcase their skills by using both their L1 and English to create bilingual projects.

Partners can collaborate to create products like short documentaries, arts-based projects, or multilingual web pages on a mutually relevant topic. Well-suited for a wide grade range and for adults, these projects should be student-centered and can be tailored to a variety of content areas and targeted learning outcomes. Aim to match your students' interests with the curriculum goals. The key to making online global collaboration a powerful and dynamic force for learning is tapping into students' previous experience and building on their existing technological and conceptual skills (Skourtou, 2002).

Find out if your school has an existing partnership with an international sister school. If not, enlist the help of colleagues or school administration to reach out to international schools and make a sister school connection. Your own students could be a valuable resource here. Families of students may have existing relationships with schools in their home countries. Invite them to be involved in the partnership project. Free video and messaging apps like WhatsApp (www.whatsapp.com) could be used to communicate with partners and organize projects. There are also numerous online resources that can be used to facilitate global partnership projects, like the following:

- epals (www.epals.com/#/connections)

- Global Encounters (tcge.tiged.org/encounters.html)

- Flipgrid (flipgrid.com)

- Belouga (belouga.org)

- Pen Pal Schools (penpalschools.com)

Pen Pal Schools, for example, is an award-winning web-based service that will match your students with pen pals from more than 150 different countries. It also has ready-to-use projects and lesson plans that can be adapted to meet individual classroom needs. Teachers can review and provide feedback for all student work online and use built-in assessment tools to align projects with a variety of assessment standards, including TEKS, Common Core, and IB standards.

The student-led nature of this work promotes feelings of ownership over both the process and the products of the collaboration, which is an integral part of literacy development (Cummins, 2005). Moreover, the positive feedback that students are likely to receive by sharing their culminating projects with multiple audiences (e.g., peers, teachers, family members, international partners, the media) can affirm their identities as intelligent, imaginative, and linguistically talented (Cummins & Early, 2011). All students in the class develop valuable 21st-century skills as they interact with students using diverse varieties of English, build cross-cultural relationships, explore notions of global citizenship, and hone digital skills.

Reimagining Instructional Materials

L2 English speakers outnumber native English speakers globally at an estimated ratio of 4:1 and growing (British Council, 2013). That the majority of English interactions today involve at least one L2 speaker means that we need far more examples of L2 user speech in the classroom. This helps both ELs and non-ELs prepare for future real-world interactions with speakers of different varieties of English. Providing models of skilled L2 English rather than strictly native speaker English is important not only to position proficient L2 user English as legitimate, but also to reflect the realities of how all students will be communicating in a globalized world. Although diverse cultural backgrounds are often represented, the situations depicted in English language and subject-specific textbooks are ones that predominantly feature native speakers modelling standard English in North American contexts.

 "Students need to be shown the richness of L2 use. Rather than a few L2 users stumbling through conversations with powerful native speakers, they need to encounter the language of people who use the language effectively as a second language, who, because they speak two languages, can say things that monolingual native speakers can never say." (Cook, 2002, p. 338)

Although there has been academic support for these ideas, there has been little impact on syllabi or assessment and, as Cook (2016) points out, "coursebooks still emphasize the roles of the powerful native speaker; the few L2 users that are mentioned are humble foreign students" (p. 187). Revising classroom materials to include examples of L2 user English and depictions of L2 users as successful members of society are necessary steps in balancing power relations and sending the message that diverse cultures, languages, and varieties of English have equal worth. Valuing ELs as talented multicompetent language users needs to be reflected in what all students hear, see, and experience in the classroom.

Do you utilize a diverse range of texts, videos, and audio in the classroom, including those that showcase L2 user English? Do you have resources that depict positive L2 user role models? Remember, there is no "neutral" approach to content—your choices send implicit messages about what is valued in the classroom and broader society. Reflect on the materials you select for new activities and reevaluate the ones in established lesson plans. If you find that most of what your students see and hear comes from native speakers of standard English, take steps to ensure you feature more diverse voices, including representations of skilled L2 user English.

It can be challenging to find examples of diverse language performances, including varied accents and dialects, to integrate into classroom learning. Enlist your students' help in collecting and creating these instructional resources. The following Practice ideas represent some of the ways you can build up a stock of L2 user resource materials and, at the same time, work toward normalizing L2 user English and pride in emerging bilingualism.

Identify, Record, and Discuss Positive L2 User Role Models (All levels)

Place students in same-L1 groups and task them with finding three examples of what they consider to be successful L2 user English by speakers from their L1 background. Students can search for resources online, on radio or television, in the wider school environment, and in communities outside of the classroom. Using mobile devices or tablets, they record short audio or video excerpts of L2 user speech—either an individual speaker or dialogue between two or more people. Upload the audio/video files and share them with the class.

Ask students to explain why they chose these examples as being representative of successful L2 user English. Discuss elements of the speech they think make it effective. As a class, discover which English skills and abilities your students most value and why. In this way, you and your students cooperatively work together as a classroom community to set appropriate goals and begin establishing L2 user norms. This activity works best in ESL classrooms, where all students are learning English as an L2.

Create Your Own Audiobook (Grades 2–6)

Tell students that they will be using digital media to create an engaging audiobook for students in kindergarten and Grade 1. Begin by showing some examples of effective audio/videobooks online (e.g., on YouTube) and prompt discussion on what good readers do; the ways that rhythm, intonation, and emphasis can help an audience to interpret the meaning of a story; how what you are reading impacts how you are reading; and the ways in which images, music, and sound effects impact the reading. Record observations and advise students to refer to these strategies when creating their own audiobooks.

Students select a book to record—one that they like and can read fluently. Give ELs the option of selecting a dual language book. Show students how to use a video creation/editing tool like iMovie (www.apple.com/imovie) or FilmoraGo (filmora .wondershare.com/filmorago-video-editing-app) to take pictures of each page in the book, record their voice, and add text and sound effects. For an easier version of this activity, simply use a tablet or mobile device to video record the book on a flat surface with the student turning the pages as they read.

Generate QR codes for each student's audiobook using a QR generator app or a website likewww.qrcode-tiger.com. Create cards that display the cover of the book next to its QR code that can be placed into kindergarten and Grade 1 classrooms for students to scan and read along. Laminate the cards for durability, hole punch them, and use a ring to keep all the stories together. This way, students can access the audiobooks easily without having to navigate the web. The audiobooks created by ELs become samples of L2 user English that can be used as models for future cohorts and younger students in the school. This activity works well in either ESL or mixed student groups (i.e., ELs and native English speakers).

Language Competence vs. Language Performance

For older students, group identity can play a role in students' language performance. It is generally assumed that when a student speaks their L1, translanguages, or uses a form of "nonstandard" English in class, it is because they are being careless or they are compensating for an inability to speak and understand Standard English. Translanguaging is actually a sophisticated language practice that reflects the dynamic and fluid nature of bilingualism, and students' language choices may reflect much more than their underlying competencies.

A multiyear study of academic performance among Indigenous children of the Gila River community found that in Grades 1–3, the children's English most resembled the standard dialect of their teacher, but by Grade 4, a time when one might expect growing competence in standard forms, their language performances increasingly began to reflect the local dialect (Nelson-Barber, 1982). These students had the ability to speak using more standard English but chose not to. The researcher believed this was due to an increased awareness of their group membership and its importance to their well-being, which was then reflected in the language choices they made. It may also have been a reaction to a growing awareness of the school's negative view of their community. It is important for educators to be aware that students may consciously choose not to use Standard English as an act of resistance against an education system that they believe devalues their language and culture while privileging monolingual, middle class social groups. They may feel that they must make a choice between identifying with their community or identifying with the school.

All students have the right to an education that gives them access to Standard English, but they also have the right to maintain and develop the language skills they bring to the classroom. This is yet another reason why there should be classroom discussions on the relationship between language and power and a focus on developing critical awareness of how ideologies lead to privilege and advantage for some and marginalization and harm for others (see Chapter 1). Understanding that difference is not deficit is critical not only for teachers but for students as well.

A Final Review and a Look to the Future

We are in the midst of a tumultuous and transformative time in history. Diversity is increasing, but so too is intolerance and anti-immigrant sentiment. Experiences of discrimination, mistreatment, and lack of belonging at school have harmful and lasting effects on students' identities, motivation, and engagement in learning. What we, as teachers, say and do in the classroom affects students' perceptions of who they are and what they are capable of at school and beyond. Our classroom policies and practices must be ones that push back against educational inequity and reinforce the value of bilingualism and multiple ways of knowing and being.

It is crucial to critically examine how we conceptualize and deliver curriculum to culturally and linguistically diverse students, including our perceptions of students' abilities as well as the standards we use to assess them. Part of this involves acknowledging that students do not emerge from the classroom into a monolingual world. They are part of a dynamic global landscape that is multicultural, multilingual, and multiliterate. On a personal level, we must adopt a plurilingual orientation that reconceptualizes L1 use in the classroom from "a regrettable fact of life that must be endured" (Cook, 2001, p. 410) into a powerful resource for learning and identity affirmation.

Toward Plurilingualism in (Language) Education

The term *plurilingual* refers to "the ways in which individuals' linguistic repertories overlap and intersect and develop in different ways with respect to languages, dialects, and registers" (Choi & Ollerhead, 2018, p. 2). Whereas multilingualism describes multiple languages existing side-by-side but being utilized separately in a given physical location or social context, plurilingualism focuses on the individual rather than the collective—the term *plurilingualism* more aptly captures the fluid, dynamic nature of languages within an individual's single integrated linguistic repertoire. It gives credence to partial skills and recognizes the cultural dimensions of language and its use. Plurilingualism accounts for a language learner's multicompetence and reflects an understanding that if a multicompetent person does not have mastery (i.e., native-like command) of a language, they are not deficient, but instead "someone who has constructive competence and thus potential to carry out tasks in various domains and situations" (Chen & Hélot, 2018, p. 172).

As our classrooms become ever more heterogenous, we can either continue to focus on fitting all students into standardized boxes or take purposeful and informed action to normalize multilingualism and value plurilingualism as an achievement. A plurilingual education signifies an inclusive, intercultural approach in the classroom, one that enables each student to assert and amplify their singularity.

Adopting a Plurilingual Orientation in the Classroom as a Force for Change

A plurilingual orientation centers on educating students bilingually, not using two languages only so long as it takes to integrate ELs into mainstream, English-only classrooms. Teachers of any subject or grade level from any language background, monolingual or polyglot, can adopt a plurilingual orientation—it is not limited to bilingual teachers in dual-language programs. It is both a mindset and an instructional trajectory, one that is about the education of students, not just about the learning of a language. Instead of positioning the native English speaker as the ultimate model to be attained, it endorses bilingual norms of English competence. It does not view bilingualism as knowing two separate, isolated languages, but as possessing a unified linguistic system that is complex and interconnected. Rather than teaching as though the L1 impedes the acquisition of academic English skills and content knowledge, a teacher with a pluri-lingual orientation adopts evidence-based asset pedagogies that valorize (even partial) competencies in more than one language, take advantage of cross-lingual transfer, build on the valuable prior knowledge encoded in the L1, and mobilize these resources to carry out classroom tasks and assignments.

Educators who embrace and actively apply this orientation to their instruction leverage students' unique funds of knowledge to enrich learning for everyone and maintain high expectations for all students. They engage themselves and their students in critical conversations that examine the inequitable power structures embedded in education and broader society that disadvantage those from diverse backgrounds. A plurilingual orientation moves toward a future of social justice. As hooks (1994) said, "the classroom, with all its limitations, remains a location of possibility" (p. 207). So, although it is crucial that we recognize the ways in which schools and classrooms (re)create difference, restrict access, and marginalize children from linguistically and culturally diverse backgrounds, it is equally important that we explore how they can also be sites of resistance and change.

REFERENCES AND FURTHER READING

America the Bilingual. (2020). *About: A few things we believe.* https://www.americathebilingual.com/about/

American Educational Research Association, American Psychological Association, & National Council on Measurement in Education. (2014). *National Council on Measurement. The standards for educational and psychological testing.* American Psychological Association.

August, D., & Shanahan, T. (Eds.). (2006). *Developing literacy in second-language learners: Report of the National Literacy Panel on language-minority children and youth.* Lawrence Erlbaum.

Baker, C. (2011). *Foundations of bilingual education and bilingualism.* Multilingual Matters.

Bialystok, E., Abutalebi, J., Bak, T. H., Burke, D. M., & Kroll, J. F. (2016). Aging in two languages: Implications for public health. *Ageing Research Reviews, 27,* 56–60. https://doi.org/10.1016/j.arr.2016.03.003

Bialystok, E., Craik, F. I., & Luk, G. (2012). Bilingualism: Consequences for mind and brain. *Trends in Cognitive Sciences, 16*(4), 240–250. https://doi.org/10.1016/j.tics.2012.03.001

Bishop, R. (2013). Indigenous and other minoritized students. In J. Hattie & A. M. Anderman (Eds.), *International guide to student achievement* (pp. 74–76). Routledge.

Bismilla, V. (2006). *Incorporation of students' first language into classroom instruction: Effects on self-esteem and academic engagement* [Qualifying research paper]. Ontario Institute for Studies in Education, University of Toronto.

Bourgoin, R. (2014). The predictive effects of L1 and L2 early literacy indicators on reading in French immersion. *Canadian Modern Language Review, 70*(3), 355–380. https://doi.org/10.3138/cmlr.2346

British Council (2013). *The English effect: The impact of English, what it's worth to the UK and why it matters.* https://www.britishcouncil.org/sites/default/files/english-effect-report-v2.pdf

Brooks-Lewis, K. A. (2009). Adult learners' perceptions of the incorporation of their L1 in foreign language teaching and learning. *Applied Linguistics, 30*(2), 216–235. https://doi.org/10.1093/applin/amn051

Bruen, J., & Kelly, N. (2014). Using a shared L1 to reduce cognitive overload and anxiety levels in the L2 classroom. *The Language Learning Journal, 45,* 368–381. https://doi.org/10.1080/09571736.2014.908405

Buriel, R., Perez, W., De Ment, T. L., Chavez, D. V., & Moran, V. R. (1998). The relationship of language brokering to academic performance, biculturalism, and self-efficacy among Latino adolescents. *Hispanic Journal of Behavioral Sciences, 20*(3), 283–297. https://doi.org/10.1177/07399863980203001

Carlo, M. S., & Sylvester, E. S. (1996). *Adult second-language reading research: How may it inform assessment and instruction?* National Center on Adult Literacy. https://doi.org/10.1037/e402602005-001

Catibusic-Finnegan, B. (2017). *Supporting multilingual children's literacy development.* Making Literacy Meaningful. http://euliteracy.eu/supporting-language-acquisition-multilingual-environments/

Centeno-Cortés, B., & Jiménez Jiménez, A. F. (2004). Problem-solving tasks in a foreign language: The importance of the L1 in private verbal thinking. *International Journal of Applied Linguistics, 14*(1), 7–35. https://doi.org/10.1111/j.1473-4192.2004.00052.x

Chen, S., Hou, Y., Benner, A., & Kim, S. Y. (2020). Discrimination, language brokering efficacy, and academic competence among adolescent language brokers. *Journal of Adolescence, 79,* 247–257. https://doi.org/10.1016/j.adolescence.2020.01.015

Chen, Y. Z., & Hélot, C. (2018). The notion of plurilingual and pluricultural competence in the teaching of foreign languages in France. *The Langscape Journal, Language Education and Multilingualism, 1,* 168–187. https://hal.archives-ouvertes.fr/hal-02090345/document

Choi, J., & Ollerhead, S. (Eds.). (2018). *Plurilingualism in teaching and learning: Complexities across contexts.* Routledge. https://doi.org/10.4324/9781315392462

Chow, P., & Cummins, J. (2003). Valuing multilingual and multicultural approaches to learning. In S. R. Schecter & J. Cummins (Eds.), *Multilingual education in practice: Using diversity as a resource* (pp. 32–61). Heinemann.

Common Core State Standards Initiative. (2020). *English language arts standards, history/social studies: Grade 9–10.* http://www.corestandards.org/ELA-Literacy/RH/9-10/

Common Core State Standards Initiative. (2020). *English language arts standards, history/social studies: Grade 11–12.* http://www.corestandards.org/ELA-Literacy/RH/11-12/

Condelli, L., Wrigley, H., & Yoon, K. S. (2009). What works for adult literacy students of English as a second language. In S. Reder, & J. Bynner (Eds.), *Tracking adult literacy and numeracy skills: Findings from longitudinal research* (pp. 132–159). Routledge.

Cook, V. (1999). Going beyond the native speaker in language teaching. *TESOL Quarterly, 33,* 2, 185–209. https://doi.org/10.2307/3587717

Cook, V. (2001). Using the first language in the classroom. *The Canadian Modern Language Review, 57*(3), 402–423. https://doi.org/10.3138/cmlr.57.3.402

Cook, V. J. (2002). Language teaching methodology and the L2 user perspective. In V. J. Cook (Ed.) *Portraits of the L2 user* (pp. 327–343). Multilingual Matters. https://doi.org/10.21832/9781853595851-015

Cook, V. (2016). Where is the native speaker now? *TESOL Quarterly, 50*(1), 186–189. https://doi.org/10.1002/tesq.286

Cook, V., & Wei, L. (Eds.). (2016). *The Cambridge handbook of linguistic multi-competence.* Cambridge University Press. https://doi.org/10.1017/cbo9781107425965

Cummins, J. (1991a). Interdependence of first-and second-language proficiency in bilingual children. In E. Bialystok (Ed.), *Language processing in bilingual children* (pp. 70–89). Cambridge University Press. https://doi.org/10.1017/cbo9780511620652.006

Cummins, J. (1991b). Language development and academic learning. In L. Malave & G. Duquette (Eds.), *Language, culture and cognition* (pp. 161–175). Multilingual Matters.

Cummins, J. (1997). Minority status and schooling in Canada. *Anthropology & Education Quarterly, 28*(3), 411–430. https://doi.org/10.1525/aeq.1997.28.3.411

Cummins, J. (2000a). *Language, power and pedagogy: Bilingual children in the crossfire.* Multilingual Matters. https://doi.org/10.21832/9781853596773

Cummins, J. (2000b). Negotiating intercultural identities in the multilingual classroom. *CATESOL Journal, 12*(1), 163–178.

Cummins, J. (2005). Teaching for cross-language transfer in dual language education: Possibilities and pitfalls. In *TESOL symposium on dual language education: Teaching and learning two languages in the EFL setting* (pp. 1–18). TESOL International Association.

Cummins, J. (2007a). Rethinking monolingual instructional strategies in multilingual classrooms. *Canadian Journal of Applied Linguistics, 10*(2), 221–240.

Cummins, J. (2007b). Research monograph #5: Promoting literacy in multilingual contexts. *What Works? Research into Practice.* The Literacy and Numeracy Secretariat, Ontario Ministry of Education.

Cummins, J. (2008). Teaching for transfer: Challenging the two solitudes assumption in bilingual education. In N. H. Hornberger (Ed.), *Encyclopedia of language and education* (pp. 65–75). https://doi.org/10.1007/978-0-387-30424-3_116

Cummins, J., Bismilla, V., Chow, P., Cohen, S., Giampapa, F., Leoni, L., Sandhu, P., & Sastri, P. (2005). Affirming identity in multilingual classrooms. *Educational Leadership, 63*(1), 38–43.

Cummins, J., & Early, M. (Eds.). (2011). *Identity texts: The collaborative creation of power in multilingual schools.* Trentham Books.

Cummins, J., Mirza, R., & Stille, S. (2012). English language learners in Canadian schools: Emerging directions for school-based policies. *TESL Canada Journal,* 25–48. https://doi.org/10.18806/tesl.v29i0.1121

de Boer, H., Timmermans, A. C., & Van Der Werf, M. P. (2018). The effects of teacher expectation interventions on teachers' expectations and student achievement: Narrative review and meta-analysis. *Educational Research and Evaluation, 24*(3–5), 180–200. https://doi.org/10.1080/13803611.2018.1550834

DeCapua, A. (2016). Reaching students with limited or interrupted formal education through culturally responsive teaching. *Language and Linguistics Compass, 10*(5), 225–237. https://doi.org/10.1111/lnc3.12183

DeCapua, A., & Marshall, H. W. (2009). Students with limited or interrupted formal education in U.S. classrooms. *The Urban Review, 42*(2), 159–173. https://doi.org/10.1007/s11256-009-0128-z

Dei, G. (2016). Decolonizing the university: The challenges and possibilities of inclusive education. *Socialist Studies/Études Socialistes, 11*(1), 23–61. https://doi.org/10.18740/s4ww31

Delpit, L. (1988). The silenced dialogue: Power and pedagogy in educating other people's children. *Harvard Educational Review, 58*(3), 280–299. https://doi.org/10.17763/haer.58.3.c43481778r528qw4

Delpit, L. (2006). *Other people's children: Cultural conflict in the classroom.* The New Press. https://doi.org/10.2307/358724

Delpit, L., & Dowdy, J. (Eds.). (2002). *The skin that we speak: Thoughts on language and culture in the classroom*. New Press.

Dorner, L., Orellana, M. F., & Li-Grining, C. P. (2007). "I helped my mom" and it helped me: Translating the skills of language brokers into improved standardized test scores. *American Journal of Education, 113*(3), 451–478. https://doi.org/10.1086/512740

Durgunoglu, A. Y., & Hughes, T. (2010). How prepared are the US preservice teachers to teach English language learners? *International Journal of Teaching and Learning in Higher Education, 22*(1), 32–41.

D'warte, J. (2014). Exploring linguistic repertoires: Multiple language use and multimodal literacy activity in five classrooms. *The Australian Journal of Language and Literacy, 37*(1), 21. https://www.researchgate.net/publication/286457408

Fillmore, L. W., & Fillmore, C. J. (2012). What does text complexity mean for English learners and language minority students? *Understanding Language: Language, Literacy, and Learning in the Content Areas* (pp. 64–74). https://ell.stanford.edu/publication/what-does-text-complexity-mean-english-learners-and-language-minority-students

Frederickson, N., & Cline, T. (2009). *Special educational needs, inclusion and diversity*. McGraw-Hill Education.

García, O. (2009). Emergent bilinguals and TESOL: What's in a name? *TESOL Quarterly, 43*(2), 322–326. https://doi.org/10.1002/j.1545-7249.2009.tb00172.x

García, O. (2017). Reflections on Turnbull's reframing of foreign language education: Bilingual epistemologies. *International Journal of Bilingual Education and Bilingualism, 22*(5), 628–638. https://doi.org/10.1080/13670050.2016.1277512

García, O., Johnson, S. I., & Seltzer, K. (2017). *The translanguaging classroom: Leveraging student bilingualism for learning*. Caslon.

García, O., Lin, A., & May, S. (Eds.). (2017). *Bilingual and multilingual education* (3rd ed.). Springer. https://doi.org/10.1007/978-3-319-02258-1

Genesee, F. (Ed.). (1994). *Educating second language children: The whole child, the whole curriculum, the whole community*. Cambridge University Press.

González, N., Moll, L. C., & Amanti, C. (Eds.). (2005). *Funds of knowledge: Theorizing practices in households, communities, and classrooms*. Lawrence Erlbaum. https://doi.org/10.4324/9781410613462

Grant, R. A., & Wong, S. D. (2008). Critical race perspectives, Bourdieu, and language education. In J. Albright & A. Luke (Eds.). *Pierre Bourdieu and literacy education* (pp. 162–184). Routledge.

Grosjean, F. (1989). Neurolinguists, beware! The bilingual is not two monolinguals in one person. *Brain and Language, 36*(1), 3–15. https://doi.org/10.1016/0093-934x(89)90048-5

Harper, C. A., & Platt, E. J. (1998). Full inclusion for secondary school ESOL students: Some concerns from Florida. *TESOL Journal, 7*(5), 30–36.

Hassapopoulou, M. (2013). Authentic hybridity: Remix and appropriation as multimodal composition. *The Journal of Interactive Technology and Pedagogy*. https://jitp.commons.gc.cuny.edu/authentic-hybridity-remix-and-appropriation-as-multimodal-composition/

Herrmann, E. (n.d.). Help or hindrance? Use of native language in the English classroom. *Multibriefs*. http://www.multibriefs.com/briefs/exclusive/help_or_hindrance.html#.iVqu5r1MrKMI

Hinnant, J. B., O'Brien, M., & Ghazarian, S. R. (2009). The longitudinal relations of teacher expectations to achievement in the early school years. *Journal of Educational Psychology, 101*, 662–670. https://doi.org/10.1037/a0014306

hooks, b. (1994). *Teaching to transgress: Education as the practice of freedom.* Routledge. https://doi.org/10.4324/9780203700280

Kroll, J. F., & Bialystok, E. (2013). Understanding the consequences of bilingualism for language processing and cognition. *Journal of Cognitive Psychology, 25*, 497–514. https://doi.org/10.1080/20445911.2013.799170

Laakso, J., & Sarhimaa, A. (2016). *Towards openly multilingual policies and practices: Assessing minority language maintenance across Europe.* Multilingual Matters.

Ladson-Billings, G. (1994). *The dreamkeepers: Successful teachers of African American children.* Jossey-Bass.

Larrivee, B. (2000). Transforming teaching practice: Becoming the critically reflective teacher. *Reflective Practice, 1*(3), 293–307. https://doi.org/10.1080/713693162

Levine, G. S. (2013). The case for a multilingual approach to language classroom communication. *Language and Linguistics Compass, 7*(8), 423–436. https://doi.org/10.1111/lnc3.12036

Lindholm-Leary, K., & Borsato, G. (2005). Hispanic high schoolers and mathematics: Follow-up of students who had participated in two-way bilingual elementary programs. *Bilingual Research Journal, 29*(3), 641–652. https://doi.org/10.1080/15235882.2005.10162856

Macaro, E. (Ed.). (2010). *The continuum companion to second language acquisition.* Continuum.

Manyak, P. C. (2004). "What did she say?" Translation in a primary-grade English immersion class. *Multicultural Perspectives, 6*, 12–18. https://doi:10.1207/ S15327892mcp0601_3

Marzecová, A., Asanowicz, D., Krivá, L., & Wodniecka, Z. (2013). The effects of bilingualism on efficiency and lateralization of attentional networks. *Bilingualism: Language and Cognition, 16*(3), 608–662. https://doi.org/10.1017/s1366728912000569

Mejía-Arauz, R., Roberts, A. D., & Rogoff, B. (2012). Cultural variation in balance of nonverbal conversation and talk. *International Perspectives in Psychology: Research, Practice, Consultation, 1*, 207–220. https://doi.org/10.1037/a0030961

Moore, T. S. (2014). *Elementary teachers' perceptions of their preparedness to teach English language learners in the mainstream classroom* (Publication No. 3608097). [Doctoral dissertation, Walden University]. ProQuest Dissertations & Theses Global.

Murphy, D. (2014, December). *The academic achievement of English language learners: Data for the U.S. and each of the states.* (Research Brief No. #2014-62). https://www.childtrends .org/wp-content/uploads/2015/07/2014-62AcademicAchievementEnglish.pdf

National Center for Education Statistics. (2020). English language learners in public schools. https://nces.ed.gov/programs/coe/indicator_cgf.asp

National Governors Association Center for Best Practices & Council of Chief State School Officers. (2010). *Common Core State Standards: English language arts & literacy in history/ social studies, science, and technical subjects (Appendix B: Text exemplars and sample performance tasks).* http://www.corestandards.org/assets/Appendix_B.pdf

Nelson-Barber, S. (1982). Phonologic variations of Pima English. In R. St. Clair & W. Leap (Eds.)., *Language renewal among American Indian tribes: Issues, problems and prospects.* National Clearinghouse for Bilingual Education.

Orellana, M. F., & García, O. (2014). Language brokering and translanguaging in school. *Language Arts, 91*(5), 386–392.

Otheguy, R., García, O., & Reid, W. (2015). Clarifying translanguaging and deconstructing named languages: A perspective from linguistics. *Applied Linguistics Review, 6*(3), 281–307. https://doi.org/10.1515/applirev-2015-0014

Palfreman, J. (Producer). (1983). A child's guide to languages (Season 20, Episode 6) [TV Series episode]. In *Horizon*. BBC. https://www.dailymotion.com/video/x7myq5y

Paradise, R., & Rogoff, B. (2009). Side by side learning by observing and pitching in: Cultural practices in support of learning. *Ethos, 37*, 102–138. https://doi.org/10.1111/j.1548-1352.2009.01033.x

Pérez, M. S., & Saavedra, C. M. (2017). A call for onto-epistemological diversity in early childhood education and care: Centering global south conceptualizations of childhood/s. *Review of Research in Education, 41*(1), 1–29. https://doi.org/10.3102/0091732x16688621

Pimentel, C., & Sevin, T. (2009). The profits of language brokering. *The Journal of Communication & Education Language Magazine, 8*(5), 16–18.

Prasad, G. L. (2015). *The prism of children's plurilingualism: A multi-site inquiry with children as co-researchers across English and French schools in Toronto and Montpellier* [Doctoral dissertation, University of Toronto].

Riedner, H. (2018). Google Translate tool makes inclusion cool at Bradford schools. *Simcoe News*. https://www.simcoe.com/news-story/8998938-google-translate-tool-makes -inclusion-cool-at-bradford-schools/

Rubie-Davies, C. M. (2008). Teacher expectations. In T. Good (Ed.), *21st century education: A reference handbook* (pp. I-254–I-265). SAGE. https://doi.org/10.4135/9781412964012.n27

Sanchez, C. (2017). *English language learners: How your state is doing*. National Public Radio Education. https://www.npr.org/sections/ed/2017/02/23/512451228/5-millionenglish -language-learners-a-vast-pool-of-talent-at-risk

Schüler-Meyer, A., Prediger, S., Kuzu, T., Wessel, L., & Redder, A. (2019). Is formal language proficiency in the home language required to profit from a bilingual teaching intervention in mathematics? A mixed methods study on fostering multilingual students' conceptual understanding. *International Journal of Science and Mathematics Education, 17*(2), 317–339. https://doi.org/10.1007/s10763-017-9857-8

Scott, V. M. (2016). Multicompetence and language teaching. In V. J. Cook & L. Wei (Eds.), *The Cambridge handbook of linguistic multicompetence* (pp. 445–461). Cambridge University Press. https://doi.org/10.1017/cbo9781107425965.021

Seven Hills Charter School. (2015). *Change the label of English language learners to multilingual students*. https://www.change.org/p/barack-obama-change-the-label-of-english-language -learners-to-multilingual-students

Skourtou, E. (2002). Connecting Greek and Canadian schools through an Internet-based sister-class network. *International Journal of Bilingual Education and Bilingualism, 5*(2), 85–95. https://doi.org/10.1080/13670050208667748

Skourtou, E., Kourtis-Kazoullis, V., & Cummins, J. (2006). Designing virtual learning environments for academic language development. In *The international handbook of virtual learning environments* (pp. 441–467). Springer. https://doi.org/10.1007/978-1-4020-3803-7_18

Sorhagen, N. S. (2013). Early teacher expectations disproportionately affect poor children's high school performance. *Journal of Educational Psychology, 105,* 465–477. https://doi.org/10.1037/a0031754

Sousa, D. A., & Tomlinson, C. A. (2011). *Differentiation and the brain: How neuroscience supports the learner-friendly classroom.* Solution Tree Press.

Souto-Manning, M. (2013). Teaching young children from immigrant and diverse families. *Young Children, 68*(4), 72.

Sparks, R. L., Patton, J., Ganschow, L., & Humbach, N. (2012). Do L1 reading achievement and L1 print exposure contribute to the prediction of L2 proficiency? *Language Learning, 62*(2), 473–505. https://doi.org/10.1111/j.1467-9922.2012.00694.x

Statistics Canada. (2020). *Number of students in official languages programs, public elementary and secondary schools, by program type, grade and sex.* https://www150.statcan.gc.ca/t1/tbl1/en/tv.action?pid=3710000901

Tavani, C. M., & Losh, S. C. (2003). Motivation, self-confidence, and expectations as predictors of the academic performances among our high school students. *Child Study Journal, 33*(3), 141–151.

TESOL International Association. (2018). *The 6 principles for exemplary teaching of English learners: Grades K–12.*

Thomas, W., & Collier, V. (2002). *A national study of school effectiveness for language minority students' long-term academic achievement.* Center for Research on Education, Diversity & Excellence.

Thomas, W. P., & Collier, V. P. (2004). The multiple benefits of dual language: Dual language programs educate both English learners and native English speakers without incurring extra costs. *Educational Leadership, 61*(2), 61–64.

Tomlinson, C. A. (2014). *The differentiated classroom: Responding to the needs of all learners.* ASCD.

U.S. Department of Education. (2018). *Academic performance and outcomes for English learners: Performance on national assessments and on-time graduation rates.* https://www2.ed.gov/datastory/el-outcomes/index.html#wrapUp

Valentino R. A., & Reardon S. F. (2015). Effectiveness of four instructional programs designed to serve English learners: Variation by ethnicity and initial English proficiency. *Educational Evaluation and Policy Analysis, 37*(4), 612–637. https://doi.org/10.3102/0162373715573310

Vasquez, V. M. (2014). *Negotiating critical literacies with young children.* Routledge. https://doi.org/10.4324/9781315848624

Vogel, S., Ascenzi-Moreno, L., & García, O. (2018). An expanded view of translanguaging: Leveraging the dynamic interactions between a young multilingual writer and machine translation software. In J. Choi & S. Ollerhead, (Eds.), *Plurilingualism in teaching and learning* (pp. 105–122). Routledge. https://doi.org/10.4324/9781315392462-6

Vogt, M. (2020). Academic language and literacy development for English learners In A. Dagen & R. Bean (Eds.), *Best practices of literacy leaders: Keys to school improvement* (pp. 325–345). Guilford Press.

Wang, W., & Wen, Q. (2002). L1 use in the L2 composing process: An exploratory study of 16 Chinese EFL writers. *Journal of Second Language Writing, 11*(3), 225–246. https://doi.org/10.1016/s1060-3743(02)00084-x

Further Reading

Acoach, C. L., & Webb, L. M. (2004). The influence of language brokering on Hispanic teenagers' acculturation, academic performance, and nonverbal decoding skills: A preliminary study. *Howard Journal of Communications*, *15*(1), 1–19. https://doi.org/10.1080/10646170490275459

Alegría de la Colina, A., & García Mayo, P. (2009). Oral interaction in task-based EFL learning: The use of the L1 as a cognitive tool. *International Review of Applied Linguistics*, *47*(3), 325–345. https://doi.org/10.1515/iral.2009.014

Bourne, J. (2001). Discourses and identities in a multi-lingual primary classroom. *Oxford Review of Education*, *27*(1), 103–114. https://doi.org/10.1080/03054980123562

Collier, V. P., & Thomas, W. P. (2004). The astounding effectiveness of dual language education for all. *NABE Journal of Research and Practice*, *2*(1), 1–20. https://www.mville.edu/sites/default/files/Dept-School%20of%20Education/Collier__Thomas_-Effectiveness_of_Dual_Language.pdf

Cook, V. (2001). Using the first language in the classroom. *Canadian Modern Language Review*, *57*(3), 402–423. https://doi.org/10.3138/cmlr.57.3.402

Cummins, J. (1979). Linguistic interdependence and the educational development of bilingual children. *Review of Educational Research*, *49*(2), 222–251. https://doi.org/10.3102/00346543049002222

Cummins, J. (2000). Academic language learning, transformative pedagogy, and information technology: Towards a critical balance. *TESOL Quarterly*, *34*(3), 537–548. https://doi.org/10.2307/3587742

Cummins, J. (2001). *Negotiating identities: Education for empowerment in a diverse society.* (2nd ed.). California Association for Bilingual Education.

Cummins, J. (2016). Reflections on Cummins (1980), "The cross-lingual dimensions of language proficiency: Implications for bilingual education and the optimal age issue." *TESOL Quarterly*, *50*(4), 940–944. https://doi.org/10.1002/tesq.339

Cummins, J., López-Gopar, M, & Sughrua, W. M. (2019). English language teaching in North American schools. In X. Gao (Ed.), *Second handbook of English language teaching* (pp. 9–29). Springer. https://doi.org/10.1007/978-3-030-02899-2_1

García, O. (2009). *Bilingual education in the 21st century: A global perspective.* Wiley/Blackwell.

Guthrie, J. T. (2004). Teaching for literacy engagement. *Journal of Literacy Research*, *36*(1), 1–30. https://doi.org/10.1207/s15548430jlr3601_2

Hirst, K., Hannon, P., & Nutbrown, C. (2010). Effects of a preschool bilingual family literacy programme. *Journal of Early Childhood Literacy*, *10*, 183–208. https://doi.org/10.1177/1468798410363838

Kerr, P. (2014). *Translation and own-language activities.* Cambridge University Press.

Lindholm-Leary, K. (2012). Success and challenges in dual language education. *Theory Into Practice*, *51*(4), 256–262. https://doi.org/10.1080/00405841.2012.726053

Lindholm-Leary, K. (2014). Bilingual and biliteracy skills in young Spanish-speaking low-SES children: Impact of instructional language and primary language proficiency. *International Journal of Bilingual Education and Bilingualism*, *17*(2), 144–159. https://doi.org/10.1080/13670050.2013.866625

Lindsay, J. (2010). *Children's access to print material and education-related outcomes: Findings from a meta-analytic review.* Learning Point.

Mandalios, J. (2013). Power and pedagogy in ELT: Native-speaker teachers and the case of bilingual dictionaries and L1. *International Journal of Applied Linguistics*, *23*, 202–225. https://doi.org/10.1111/j.1473-4192.2012.00326.x

Marian, V., Shook, A., & Schroeder, S. R. (2013). Bilingual two-way immersion programs benefit academic achievement. *Bilingual Research Journal*, *36*(2), 167–186. https://doi.org/10.1080/15235882.2013.818075

McCarty, T. L. (2005). *Language, literacy, and power in schooling*. Routledge. https://doi.org/10.4324/9781410613547

Menken, K. (2013). Restrictive language education policies and emergent bilingual youth: A perfect storm with imperfect outcomes. *Theory into Practice*, *52*(3), 160–168. https://doi.org/10.1080/00405841.2013.804307

Menken, K., & Avni, S. (2019). Language policy conflicts: New York City's efforts to expand bilingual education midst English-only pressures. In T. Ricento (Ed.), *Language Politics and Policies: Perspectives from Canada and the United States* (pp. 153–172). Cambridge University Press. http://dx.doi.org/10.1017/9781108684804.009

Menken, K., & Solorza, C. (2014). No child left bilingual: Accountability and the elimination of bilingual education programs in New York City schools. *Educational Policy*, *28*(1), 96–125. https://doi.org/10.1177/0895904812468228

Nation, P. (2003). The role of the first language in foreign language learning. *Asian EFL Journal*, *1*, 35–39. https://doi.org/10.26686/wgtn.12560333.v1

Olssen, M. (Ed.). (2006). *Culture and learning: Access and opportunity in the classroom*. Information Age.

Pimentel, C. (2011). The color of language: The racialized educational trajectory of an emerging bilingual student. *Journal of Latinos and Education*, *10*(4), 335–353. https://doi.org/10.1080/15348431.2011.605686

Sánchez, M. T., García, O., & Solorza, C. (2018). Reframing language allocation policy in dual language bilingual education. *Bilingual Research Journal*, *41*(1), 37–51. https://www.gocabe.org/wp-content/uploads/2019/12/sanchezreframing-language -allocation-policy-in-dual-language-bilingual-education-34.pdf https://doi.org/10.1080 /15235882.2017.1405098

Swain, M., & Lapkin, S. (2000). Task-based second language learning: The uses of the first language. *Language Teaching Research*, *4*(3), 251–274. https://doi.org/10.1191/136216800125087

Thomas, W., & Collier, V. (1997). *School effectiveness for language minority students*. National Clearinghouse for Bilingual Education.

Tse, L. (1995). Language brokering among Latino adolescents: Prevalence, attitudes, and school performance. *Hispanic Journal of Behavioral Sciences*, *17*(2), 180–193. https://doi.org/10.1177/07399863950172003

Tse, L. (1996). Language brokering in linguistic minority communities: The case of Chinese- and Vietnamese-American students. *Bilingual Research Journal*, *20*(3–4), 485–498. https://doi.org/10.1080/15235882.1996.10668640

INDEXES, APPENDIXES, AND RESOURCES

Appendixes can be found online at this book's companion website:
www.tesol.org/homelanguage

Index 1: Practice Items

Index 2: Reflection Questions

- Do you think it is important for English learners (ELs) to maintain and develop their home language (L1) as they learn English? If so, why? If not, why not? Return to this question when you have finished reading this guidebook. Notice and reflect on any changes to your original position.

- Do your classroom policies and instructional strategies reflect an understanding of languages as interdependent or as separate from one another in the cognitive system?

- Using Cummins's (2005) five types of cross-lingual transfer (see p. 11), brainstorm five instructional strategies and/or activities you could use in your classroom to take advantage of each (one strategy/activity for each type of transfer).

- *Step 1*: What is your personal teacher identity? Free-write for 10 minutes on how you define your role as an educator of culturally and linguistically diverse students. What do you expect of yourself and your students? What are your intentions, assumptions, and goals?

- *Step 2*: Read what you wrote and think about how the various expectations, assumptions, and goals you bring to the task of educating these students shapes your interactions with them. Reflect on ways your teacher identity might act to either constrict or extend your students' identities and learning.

- Think about a high-performing student and a low-performing student you have or have had in the past. If you are a preservice teacher, consider asking a practicing teacher these questions, or think about experiences you have had in your student teaching:

  — Where did your expectations for each student come from (e.g., discussions with the students' previous teachers; classroom behavior; biases you may have about their race, class, language background)?

  — How did your expectations and underlying beliefs affect your interactions with those students?

  — Did you give them equal opportunities to learn and demonstrate learning?

  — If not, how could you have done better?

- How would you reimagine a lesson or unit you teach through a social justice lens? What modifications or extensions could you use that harness students' language resources and prior knowledge (*the how*) to support them in meeting curriculum standards (*the what*)?

- Why might you encourage L1 use? Have you ever encouraged students to use their L1 in the classroom? What benefits did you find? Do you have any concerns about allowing ELs to use their L1? Think of some ways that you could mitigate any perceived negative effects.

- After reading the scenario on pp. 35–36, ask yourself: What may have helped you in this scenario? What may have been difficult in this scenario? Pausing to empathize with the everyday challenges your ELs encounter in the classroom on a regular basis will help you to make strategic and caring instructional decisions around the use of their L1.

- Think about a concept in the curriculum that is abstract. Consider that for many students with limited or interrupted formal education, learning is experiential—for many of these students, learning happens in a real-world context, so decontextualized content may present a challenge. How could you create some context (i.e., immediate relevance) to provide support for students to achieve the same learning objective for your lesson using a different path to get there (i.e., framing the problem differently or using a different process)?

- If you heard students translanguaging in your classroom, would your immediate reaction be positive or negative? Think about the situation from an asset-based perspective—is there a way to extend students' translanguaging practices to make connections to the curriculum? If so, how? If not, why not?

- Record samples of dialogue between you and one of your ELs when you are working on an academic task in the classroom and when you are having a casual conversation outside of class. What differences do you notice? Does the student have trouble understanding any of the language in the classroom? What do you do to help the student fully understand the content and/or instructions in the classroom? How could you support them more effectively?

- Examining and naming our assumptions, judgements, and expectations related to diverse students is a crucial part of reflecting on practice and enacting more equitable instruction. Harvard University's Project Implicit (implicit.harvard.edu/implicit) has a variety of Implicit Association Tests designed to measure an individual's implicit biases—attitudes and beliefs that people may be unwilling or unable to report. This test can be taken online by anyone and can reveal if you have an implicit attitude that you did not know about.

- "... Teachers, researchers, and people in general have often taken for granted that L2 learners represent a special case that can be properly judged by the standards of another group. Grammar that differs from native speakers', pronunciation that betrays where L2 users come from, and vocabulary that differs from native usage are treated as signs of L2 users' failure to become native speakers, not of their accomplishments in learning to use the L2" (Cook, 1999, pp. 194–195). Cook (2002) defines an L2 user as a person who uses another language for any purpose at whatever level, arguing that "L2 learner" is a term that implies the person is always learning, never achieving. ELs are not monolingual native English speakers, so do you agree with Cook that they should not be expected to conform to the norms of a group to which they do not belong? In your instruction, how could you integrate a focus on these students' achievements as users of more than one language rather than their perceived deficits when compared to native English speakers?

- Do you utilize a diverse range of texts, videos, and audio in the classroom, including those that showcase L2 user English? Do you have resources that depict positive L2 user role models? Remember, there is no "neutral" approach to content—your choices send implicit messages about what is valued in the classroom and broader society. Reflect on the materials you select for new activities and reevaluate the ones in established lesson plans. Next time you are gathering resources for a lesson, make an effort to find representations that reflect your students' identities back to them in a positive light.

Appendix A: Online Resources

The following list supplements the many online resources already included throughout the book, with several additional practical and conceptual resources for integrating students' home languages into instruction and supporting the development of educational policies that provide equitable educational opportunities for all students.

CUNY-New York State Initiative on Emergent Bilinguals (NYSIEB)'s YouTube Channel: This channel includes a wealth of useful resources including a webseries called "Teaching Bilinguals (Even If You're Not One)" that follows Research Assistant Sara Vogel on a journey across New York to learn how teachers harness their students' diverse language practices as valuable resources for learning. (www.youtube.com/channel/UC5PE-qUgT9LHiYq6yuVJ1fw)

Content-Area Bilingual Glossaries: These are available for free online in a variety of languages. (research.steinhardt.nyu.edu/metrocenter/resources/glossaries)

2lingual: This Google-powered site allows you to search the internet in two languages simultaneously. Available in 37 languages, search results are presented side-by-side. (www.2lingual.com)

Online Dictionaries: WordReference.com (www.wordreference.com) and Linguee (www.linguee.com) are both online bilingual dictionaries that provide context-rich translations.

Platform of Resources and References For Plurilingual and Intercultural Education: The Council of Europe provides information and resources to help educators to develop curriculum that accounts for all of the languages present in the school and promote equitable access to quality education. (www.coe.int/en/web/language-policy/platform)

WorldStories: This free online resource features an extensive collection of stories from around the world in a variety of languages and includes translations, pictures, and sound recordings. (worldstories.org.uk)

Unite For Literacy: This free and easy-to-use resource provides digital access to hundreds of picture books, with narrations in 40+ languages. (uniteforliteracy.com)

The Dual-Language Showcase: This site from Thornwood Public School has numerous dual-language books created by students in 28 different languages and includes a description of the project with stated benefits and goals. (schools.peelschools.org/1363/DualLanguage/Documents/index.htm)

Teaching the Language of Schooling in the Context of Diversity: This website contains several resources and various study materials for teachers, including activities that build on students' plurilingualism. (maledive.ecml.at/Home/tabid/3598/language/en-GB/Default.aspx)

The Seal of Biliteracy: This seal can be attached to a student's diploma when they have reached proficiency in two or more languages. This website can tell you if you are in a state that has adopted the seal and provide information on how to advocate for it if you are not. (www.sealofbiliteracy.org)

Appendix B: Personal Teacher Identity Reflection Tool

Step 1: Free-write for 10 minutes on the question/prompts provided.

What is your role as a teacher of culturally and linguistically diverse students?

Prompts: What do you expect of yourself as an educator?
What do you expect of your students? Do you have different expectations for different students?
What are your short-term (day-to-day) and long-term (for the future) goals for student learning?
What do you do in the classroom to accomplish them?

Step 2: Read and reflect on what you wrote. Think about how the various expectations, assumptions, and goals you bring to the task of educating culturally and linguistically diverse students shape your interactions with them. Consider:

- How might your teacher identity work to support and extend your students' identity and learning?

- How might your teacher identity work to undermine or constrict your students' identity and learning?

Appendix C: Plurilingual Lesson Planning Template

Standard	Bilingual Teaching Strategies	Link to Standard
e.g. CCSS.ELA-LITERACY.RL.6.4 Determine the meaning of words and phrases as they are used in a text, including figurative and connotative meanings; analyze the impact of a specific word choice on meaning and tone.	Group students with the same language background to discuss the text (e.g., contextual clues) using any language(s). Encourage them to find L1 equivalents for the key word(s) or phrase(s) and translate the surrounding sentence.	By explicitly making connections to L1, students can draw on prior conceptual knowledge and more efficiently acquire the language (label) for those concepts in English. Use of L1 clarifies meaning and aids in grappling with complex text.

Appendix D: Plurilingual Unit Planning Template

Unit Plan Title:	
Curriculum Frame Essential Question Unit Questions	
Content Standards	

Learning Outcomes Content & Language Objectives	Objectives Across Languages Language-Specific Objectives
Culminating Project	**Other Assessment Opportunities**
Texts and/or Resources In Home Language	In English

Appendix E: Promoting an Inclusive Multilingual Classroom Checklist

Instructions: Check off items that you already do in your classroom. Identify gaps and consider taking action to address them; check them off as you do.

☐ Know your students' language backgrounds (i.e., get information from the Home Language Survey, engage them in an initial conversation about their language[s]).

☐ Pair new ELs with a peer mentor to help guide them through classroom routines and activities. If possible, pair same-L1 students together or provide mentors who do not speak their mentees' L1 with a machine translator.

☐ Ask students or families to create a short welcome message in their L1 at the beginning of the year to post in the classroom.

☐ Exhibit multilingual work on classroom walls (e.g., students' bilingual work, multilingual word walls, poetry or art using languages other than English).

☐ Post classroom signs and labels in students' L1s.

☐ Encourage families to send in artwork, pictures, or other artifacts to display in the classroom. These can be specific to a particular unit of study or items that will be posted all year round.

☐ Engage students in classroom activities that use their L1.

☐ Provide opportunities during lessons or in culminating projects to showcase students' bilingual skills.

☐ Work with your school librarian to select books or resources in the L1s of your students that relate to curricular themes you are studying.

☐ Invite guest speakers from diverse cultural and linguistic backgrounds, including family members of students, to speak to the class.

☐ Create collaborative (multilingual) classroom contracts that involve students in classroom decision-making.

☐ Send home classroom communication in students' L1 whenever possible.

☐ Create opportunities to discuss, compare, and analyze different languages and language varieties (e.g., ask students to teach the class how to say something from their L1 and compare with equivalences in other languages, including English).

☐ Provide students access to online translation tools if possible (e.g., on a phone or tablet) to help facilitate classroom learning and peer/teacher interaction for early emergent ELs.

☐ Initiate and maintain dialogue with families that focuses on the importance of both L1 maintenance and development and English development.

☐ Involve parents or caregivers in their child's education regardless of their language or literacy proficiency (e.g., have students collaborate with parents to create dual-language texts, send home books in L1 for families to read together, invite parents to attend bilingual performances at school).

Note: EL = English learner; L1 = home language.

Appendix F: Student (Plurilingual) Performance by Task

Instructions: Use this form to keep track of your students' performances on specific tasks using their full language repertoire. Be sure to take note of the nature of the task (e.g., journal writing, creating a Venn diagram in groups, pair and share about a personal experience). Link these tasks and performances to content standards to gain insight into whether students are meeting expectations (in any of: English, home language [L1], or a combination thereof).

Student Name	Task	Performance Using English	Performance Using L1	Performance Using Both English and L1	Standard (Optional)

*Use categories of assessment/progression that make sense to you (e.g., beginning, emerging, progressing, independent, proficient)

Appendix G.1: Student Self-Assessment Tool

Name:

1. What did I learn? (What questions can I now answer?)

2. The most interesting work I did was ...

   The most challenging work I did was ...

3. I used English for ...

   I used my home language for ...

4. My home language helped me in my learning because ...

5. I learned the following vocabulary and/or language structures (in either English or home language):

6. I demonstrated what I learned by ...

7. What did I do well?

   What am I still learning?

8. I achieved some / most / all of the criteria.

9. I have these new questions about the topic:

10. My goal for the next month is ...

Appendix G.2: Student Self-Assessment Tool (Spanish-English)

Name:

1. ¿Qué aprendi? (¿Qué preguntas puedo ahora contester?) / What did I learn? (What questions can I now answer?)

2. El trabajo más interesante que hice fue … / The most interesting work I did was …

   El trabajo más difícil que hice fue … / The most challenging work I did was …

3. Usé inglés para … / I used English for …

   Usé español para … / I used Spanish for …

4. Español me ayudó en mi aprendizaje porque … / Spanish helped me in my learning because …

5. Aprendí el siguiente vocabulario y/o estructuras del lenguaje (en inglés o español) /
   I learned the following vocabulary and/or language structures (in either English or Spanish):

6. Demostré lo que aprendí … / I demonstrated what I learned by …

7. ¿Qué hice bien? / What did I do well?

   ¿Qué sigo aprendiendo? / What am I still learning?

8. Logré alguno / la mayoría / todos los criterios. / I achieved some / most / all of the criteria.

9. Tengo estas nuevas preguntas sobre el tema: / I have these new questions about the topic:

10. Mi objetivo para el próximo mes es … / My goal for the next month is …